ISBN 978-1-334-20325-1
PIBN 10755904

This book is a reproduction of an important historical work. Forgotten Books uses state-of-the-art technology to digitally reconstruct the work, preserving the original format whilst repairing imperfections present in the aged copy. In rare cases, an imperfection in the original, such as a blemish or missing page, may be replicated in our edition. We do, however, repair the vast majority of imperfections successfully; any imperfections that remain are intentionally left to preserve the state of such historical works.

Table of Contents

EEDLEWORK has been a most fascinating and profitable pastime from time immemorial, yet there is seldom a year passes that does not bring forth several new and interesting books or pamphlets — the subject being apparently inexhaustible.   In preparing this volume the object has been to present a number of original designs, simple yet artistic, which can be easily reproduced by the average needleworker.

The working directions are clear and explicit, and by the aid of the numerous illustrations of stitches and designs, a practical knowledge of Sewing, Crocheting, Embroidery, Knitting, Darning and Tatting, may be readily obtained, even by those who have received no previous instruction.

It is hoped that needleworkers of all ages will have pleasure and satisfaction in reproducing the many beautiful and durable articles of fancywork described within these pages, and that the book will be of special service to those just beginning to sew or to do fancywork.

Plain Sewing

AS THE stitches used in plain sewing are the foundation of every kind of needlework, it is well for the girl who wishes to learn how to make her own clothes or to embroider, first to master the several stitches used in sewing by hand. It is very necessary to have working materials of the best, for with inferior needles that bend and snap, or thread that knots and breaks, it is next to impossible to do good work. Never use a bent needle, or one that has a rough, uneven eye which will fray and cut the thread. Medium length needles are the best for white work, long ones for dressmaking, and still longer ones, with long eyes, for darning. Needles with long eyes, known as crewel needles, should also be used for embroidery.

For women who have difficulty in threading the ordinary needle, calyx-eyed needles will come as a boon. A pressure with the thread on the top of the needle will open the eye and thread the needle. Calyx-eyed and other styles of needles suitable for plain sewing and embroidery, are illustrated on page 96 of this book.

Most beginners make the mistake of using a thread that is too long; this is especially true in white sewing, where a thread eighteen or twenty inches in length is quite sufficient for everything except basting. Do not use a knot in starting a thread, except in basting or sewing a seam; in other instances fasten the thread with two or three tiny back stitches.

It is necessary to learn at least four simple stitches in order to sew well by hand. The first, illustrated at Fig. 1, is called a running stitch. Pass the needle in and out of the material in a horizontal direction, always making the stitches the same size. Where the material will permit it, several stitches may be taken up on the needle at once before pulling it through (see Fig. 1). Running stitch is used for plain seams, for joining light materials and for making gathers.

Back-stitching, shown in the second illustration, is worked from right to left. As will be seen by referring to the detail, the stitch on the right side of the material is only half the length of that on the wrong side; this is accomplished by always bringing the needle out at a point beyond the spot where it was last drawn out. Now that

O.N.T.

almost everyone owns a sewing machine, back-stitching is not used as frequently as in the past, when every-thing—no matter what the material—was sewed by hand. Back stitch is frequently used in combination with

Fig. 1

running stitch in sewing a seam. By taking a back stitch after every three or four running stitches, the seam is less likely to rip.

A detail of plain hemming is shown at Fig. 3. To insure an even hem, draw a thread from the material and cut on this line. Fold down the raw edge as narrow as possible, then fold the material a second time, sewing on the folded edge. Insert the needle and fasten thread under the fold; then, pointing the needle toward the left in a slanting direction, take up a few threads of the material below the fold, bringing the needle out through the edge of the fold (see illustration).

In making rolled hems on lingerie and children's clothes the edge of the material is rolled between the thumb and first finger of the right hand, working from right to left. The folded or rolled edge should be less than one-sixteenth of an inch wide and the needle must be slipped in so as to go only through the first turning in order that no stitches will show on the right side. When lace is to be used as a finish it may be sewed on at the same time that the hem is rolled, thus saving time and making a less clumsy edge. In setting in lace insertion it is advisable to hem the edges down to the material; then, turning the garment on to the wrong side, cut the material away from beneath the lace, leaving only a narrow edge on each side. Then roll and whip these raw edges, taking the stitches through the insertion as well as the material, thus making the lace doubly firm.

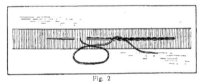

Fig. 2

O.N.T.

Fig. 3 Hemming

Convent hemming, shown at Fig. 4, used for table linen, is more like overhanding than plain hemming. A hem is laid as described for plain hemming, then the damask is again creased down on a line with the folded edge. Begin at the left-hand corner and take a straight stitch through the two folded edges, making the succeeding stitches less than one-sixteenth of an inch apart. The thread must not be drawn too tight, lest, when the hem is finished and flattened with the thimble, it will not lie perfectly flat.

Overhanding, shown in Fig. 5, is worked from right to left. This stitch is chiefly used for joining the two edges of material together. In overhanding selvage edges, one must be equally careful not to pull the thread too tight so that the seam will lie perfectly flat when finished and smoothed out. Pieces of lace edging and insertion should always be overhanded together, and if done well it should be almost impossible to see the joining stitches.

Overcasting, which is sometimes confused with overhanding, is worked in the same way, but the stitches are taken much further apart. It is only used to prevent the cut or raw edge of a material from fraying, consequently the work may be done more or less roughly.

In making underwear or children's clothes where a fine, narrow seam is desired, work as shown in Fig. 6. This is called a French seam and is made as follows: Run the two pieces of material together, placing the wrong sides together and the

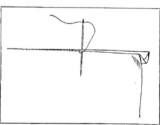

Fig. 4 Convent Hemming

edges perfectly even. This completed, trim the edges quite close, then fold the material over so that the right sides come together inside with the raw edges between. Now run the two pieces of material together again, stitching just below the edge of the inside seam (see illustration).

Gathers are made with running stitches of exactly the same length set in a straight line. Instead of holding the material fast with the left thumb, push it on the needle, taking five or six stitches before pulling the needle all the way through. When the gathering thread has been run all the way across, drop it and holding the material between the thumb and forefinger of the left hand, stroke the gathers into place. This is done with a coarse needle, stroking it down between the gathers, and slipping each gather along under the left thumb after it is stroked.

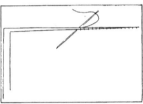

Fig. 5   Overhanding

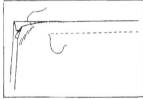

Fig. 6   French Seam

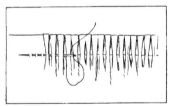

Fig. 7   Gathering

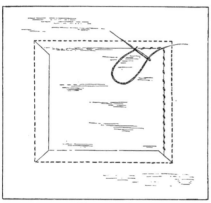

The way to patch

Mending

Though few people really enjoy patching or darn-ing, the fact remains that most women have it to do, to a greater or lesser extent. Few girls are taught how to mend, so one is sometimes inclined to think that possibly the distaste for repairing of all kinds is due largely to a lack of knowledge of the correct way to set to work, rather than to an actual dislike for the task itself. In patching one may employ one or more of the plain sewing stitches, viz: Back-stitching, hem-ming or overhanding, but darning employs but one stitch and that stitch is for the most part worked in but one way.

Where the material is too torn to stand darning it must be cut away and replaced by a new piece. In the case of underwear or cotton garments of any kind, it is advisable that the new piece should be of a lighter weight than the garment itself. Cut the patch by the line of the thread and about an inch larger each way than the hole it is to cover. Tack in the new piece so that its edges overlap the edges of the hole. The back-stitching must be done on the garment itself, it being easier then to do the corners neatly. Turn the hem down 'onto the patch, making a little snip at each corner to prevent puckering, then hem down the folded edge.

O.N.T.

A Stocking Darn

On woolen goods the edges of the hole should be left uneven and darned down to the patch, using thread of the material for the darning, whenever this is possible. Do not try to turn in the edges of the patch either, but instead darn down smoothly on to the material, taking the stitches quite close together.

When only a few of the warp or woof threads are torn or missing, a darn will replace them, providing the surrounding parts are in good condition.

One of the reasons why so few people darn stockings really well is because they try to keep the darn small. By so doing the threads are very apt to tear through the thin part of the stocking the first time it is washed and then the darn must be done over. If the thread is darned back and forth through the worn part surrounding the hole, being sure to leave loops at each turning to allow for shrinking in washing, the result will be a smooth, flat darn which will wear as long as the rest of the stocking.

Darning should always be done on the wrong side of the material and care must be taken that the thread is of a suitable weight. Thread that is too heavy makes an ugly, clumsy darn and one which is apt to pull out, while if the thread be too fine it adds considerably to the work. The Clark's O. N. T. 4 Strand Cotton, large balls, comes in white and black only, and is particularly recommended because of its softness and superior finish, but one can get small balls of this 4 Strand Cotton or small spools of plain finish Darning Cotton in a large range of colors, so there is no excuse for using cotton which does not match the material. Two or three strands make a sufficiently heavy thread for stockings and thin underwear, while three or even all four threads may be used if the underwear is heavy.

Most people find that a darning ball or gourd makes stocking darning easier; one may be purchased for a few cents from any dealer carrying needlework supplies. For fine materials, such as chiffon, lace or batiste, it is advisable to baste carefully the torn place over a piece of moderately stiff paper. so that it cannot slip out of place.

O.N.T.

A Few of the Popular Embroidery Stitches

Outline Stitch

Cat-Stitch

The ability to sew neatly is a distinct advantage to the girl who wishes to learn to embroider, for the mere fact of knowing how to place the needle so that the stitches are accurate and evenly spaced seems to make it easy to acquire the skill necessary for successful embroidery,

It is always surprising to the accomplished needlewoman to find that so few fancy stitches are known to the self-taught embroiderer, and though books on embroidery in all its forms have been published by the score, one sees, in most instances, not more than three or four stitches utilized in working out the "popular" designs of today.

Good materials and adequate utensils are as much a necessity for embroidery as for plain sewing and one must be sure to have a paper of crewel needles in assorted sizes, sharp pointed scissors and a pair of well-padded hoops or rings before beginning to work. While sewing needles may be used, the long-eyed crewel needle will be found much more convenient, especially for the stranded cotton that is so much used.

The first-learned and simplest embroidery stitches, such as outlining, chain and feather stitch, do not require the use of hoops, in fact they can be worked to better advantage when the material is held in the hand. As one advances, however, and begins the more elaborate stitches—French knots, seeding, Turkish stitch, etc., etc.—the material should always be placed in the hoop before beginning to work.

Some stitches require part of the work to be done with the material stretched in the hoop and completed with the work held in the hand. Take, for instance, buttonholing or scalloping. When the scallops are padded the filling or padding should always be done in the hoop, but the buttonhole stitch can be made much more accurately and rapidly with the work held in the hand. The same directions hold good for satin-stitch or French embroidery, while for eyelet work no hoops are needed.

Chain Stitch

O.N.T.

Outline Stitch—Fasten thread at the beginning of line to be covered; take up a stitch on the line about an eighth of an inch from the starting point. Take up the next stitch about an eighth of an inch from the last and continue working in this way until the outline is finished. Always keep the thread on the same side of the needle; if this is not done the line will be rough and uneven.

Turkish Stitch

Chain Stitch—Fasten thread at top of line; take up a straight stitch, throwing thread under the needle and in this way making a loop. Take up another straight stitch, putting the needle into the material as close as possible to the spot where the thread was brought out; throw thread under needle and pull through. Chain stitch is always worked toward you and when correctly done should look like the wrong side of the stitch made with a single thread machine.

Cat-Stitch—This stitch is worked from left to right. Fasten the thread at the top, take a stitch on the line below, pointing the needle toward the left; then take a stitch on the top line, next on the lower line and continue in this way. When the stitches are taken very close together cat-stitch is known as Turkish stitch.

Seeding—This stitch is much used in working up monograms in order to lighten the heavy effect produced by the satin-stitch, but it is equally effective on centerpieces or pillow tops in combination with other fancy stitches.

Seeding

Seeding is always worked back and forth in rows, the stitches being about three-sixteenths of an inch apart. By referring to the illustration it will be seen that the seed effect is gained by a series of back stitches, the stitches in the second and succeeding rows being taken between those of the row preceding. To be effective the stitches must be uniform in size and the rows equal distances apart.

Buttonhole Stitch—The illustration shows clearly how the buttonholing is done, as well as the method of padding or filling so that the scallop will present a raised effect. Where

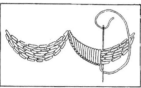

Buttonholing

padding is not required, the lower line of the scallop may be covered with a running stitch which will serve to prevent the material from fraying or tearing in laundering.

If preferred, plain or chain outline may be used instead of the running stitch, but the padding must always be worked in the opposite direction from the buttonhole stitches.

French Knots—Fasten the thread firmly, then, holding the needle in the right hand, wind the thread around the needle three or four times and put needle through to wrong side as near as possible to the spot where it was brought out. Hold the thread or silk with the left hand until it is pulled all the way through; this prevents the wound thread from slipping or knotting. French knots are more easily made when the material is stretched in an embroidery hoop or frame, the size of the knot being determined by the number of times the thread is wound around the needle.

Featherstitch—This stitch is used most often on underwear and infants' and children's clothes; it is a variation of buttonhole stitch and really simple and easy to do, though it takes practice before one can make a straight and even line.

Begin by fastening the thread at the top of the line, take a short, diagonal buttonhole stitch at the right side, bringing the needle through near the center line. Take the next stitch at the left side, somewhat lower down, again bringing the needle out at center. Continue working in this way from side to side. A stitch which is very feathery in effect is known as V-stitch; this is most often used on conventional designs or figures showing a center vein or mid-rib. Begin by taking a straight stitch about three-sixteenths of an inch long from tip of petal into center, bringing needle

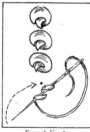

French Knots

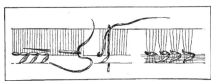

Hemstitching

out at left side, close to top of straight stitch. Put the needle in at the right side directly opposite, bringing it through to the right side of material in the center of the petal just below the straight stitch, throwing the thread under the needle, thus forming a pointed or V-stitch; again put the needle down to the wrong side, sewing this V-stitch down with a tiny seed stitch. Continue working this way leaving enough space in the center between stitches so that the seed stitches show plainly.

Hemstitching—This stitch is used as a finish to scarf ends, square centerpieces or doilies and on infants' and children's clothes, between groups of tucks and as a finish for the lower edge. The bands of hemstitching may be wide or narrow, according to the number of threads that are drawn out. The threads must be pulled out of the material just below the folded edge of the hem and it is advisable to baste the latter firmly, so that it will not slip. Fasten the thread at the left and slip the needle from right to left under four or five threads; draw it through and pull it down and through one of two threads of the folded edge. Continue taking stitches in this way until the entire hem is hemstitched.

A more elaborate openwork effect may be produced by turning the work around and making a second row of stitches on the other edge of the material, taking up the same threads as in the first row. This forms little perpendicular bars like the rungs of a ladder and is called ladder hemstitch.

Serpentine hemstitch, another variation which is pretty and easy to do, is begun in the same way as plain or ladder hemstitch. In the second or return row of hemstitching, however, instead of taking up the same group of threads, take half of one group and half of the next as one stitch, thus dividing the bars. Continue working in this way all across, producing a zigzag or serpentine effect.

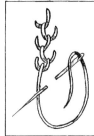

Feather Stitching

O.N.T.

French Embroidery
Showing Monograms of Various Styles

No matter how many or varied the styles of needlework may be which are presented each season to the embroiderer, there never will be, any permanent supplanting of the beautiful solid white work known as French embroidery. True, it takes time and much practice before one can attempt any but the simplest of patterns, but, on the other hand, the piece, once completed, will outwear most of the so-called novelties, while frequent laundering serves but to renew its freshness.

The secret of successful satin-stitch or solid embroidery lies in the padding or filling. When this is correctly done, with stitches that run in the same direction and rows that lie smooth and even, the satin-stitch itself will present but few difficulties even to a beginner. Padding should always be worked with the material stretched smoothly in a frame or hoop or it may be basted on a piece of rather stiff paper and the work done while on the paper. Satin-stitch is not always padded, but the French embroidery designs, when worked out, generally show the figures standing out from the linen in more or less high relief.

The padding or filling may be done in an uneven darning stitch, outlining or chain-stitch. according to the shape and size of the space to be filled. In any case it must be worked so that it will lie directly opposite or at right angles to the "over and over" or satin-stitch. The latter must be worked carefully with stitches that lie close and even but never on top of one another. The fault which is most noticeable in the satin-stitch done by non-professionals, is its tendency to break or crack if the work is folded or bent. This will not occur if the padding is firm and the over-and-over stitches are taken sufficiently close together.

O.N.T.

Most amateur embroiderers make the mistake of using too fine a thread for their French embroidery. Clark's O. N. T. Coton a Broder comes in twelve different sizes, running from No. 8 to No. 60, but it is an exceptionally fine piece of work that requires the use of a cotton huer than size 40. For the ordinary centerpiece or lingerie design, size 25 or 30 will generally be found to be fine enough for the satin-stitch, while 16, 18 or 20 may be used for the filling. Many needleworkers are satisfied with the white plain finish darning cotton for padding, but the same cotton that is used for the embroidery stitches is generally preferred.

Modern designs for French embroidery frequently introduce some open or eyelet figures as a contrast to the heavy solid work, and the effect gained by the combination of the two styles of embroidery is usually pleasing.

Eyelet work, or Madeira embroidery as it is generally called, is far easier to learn to do well than is satin-stitch, for the knack of pulling the thread so that the stitches lie snug and close is soon acquired. No matter what the size or shape of the eyelet may be, round, oval or bead-like, the outline must always be covered with a running stitch. Use the same thread that is to be used for the eyelet work, and when the outline is completed begin the over-and-over stitch without breaking the thread. Small round eyelets may be punched with a stiletto, but oval eyelets and large round ones must be cut lengthwise and crosswise and again between, if necessary, and the edges folded back to the wrong side. Then begin to work the over-and-over stitches over the double or folded edge, trimming off the edges of the material on the wrong side when the eyelet is completed. Detail illustrations of eyelet work are shown on page 19.

O.N.T.

Stem stitch or satin outline is made by covering ordinary outlining with tiny over-and-over stitches, thus producing a smooth, satiny line. One needs considerable practice before an even, unbroken line can be worked, and for that reason comparatively few amateurs attempt it, except on very fine designs where a plain outline stitch would be out of place.

Scalloping or buttonholing is a stitch which practically everyone knows how to do, and yet there are comparatively few women who can buttonhole a scalloped edge really well. The reason for this lies in the fact that buttonholing must be worked quite firm and close, the back of the stitch, in particular, being pulled up tight. Where padding is used, care must be taken to narrow it down at the joining of the scallops, so that they will still be shapely after the buttonholing is completed.

It is only after much practice that one can successfully work initials or monograms on underwear or household linen, for there is no other form of embroidery in which accuracy of stitchery is so necessary. Initialing appears to present greater difficulties than do the most elaborate floral figures, and it is generally necessary to take a few lessons from an expert before one can be sure of the correct method of working.

There are two essential points to be observed when selecting a design for a monogram; the first is that the combination of letters be graceful and artistic and the second that it be clear and readable. A monogram which is almost illegible is valueless.

In working a monogram it is frequently desirable to vary the stitchery of the different initials, not only to emphasize distinctness but also to enhance the artistic effect. The surname initial is always the largest in a three-letter monogram, while the other two initials may be of the same size or one letter may be smaller than the other.

The correct size for a letter on a large table cloth or sheet varies from three to four inches, according to personal taste. Napkins may be marked with letters from half an inch to an inch and a half in height, while pillow cases require a letter or monogram one half the size of the one used on the sheet.

Towels may be marked with two-inch letters placed from one-and-a-half to two inches above the hem.

O.N.T.

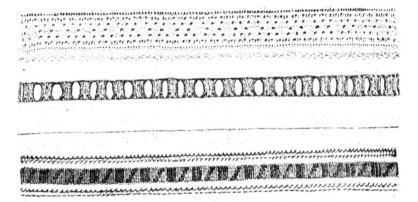

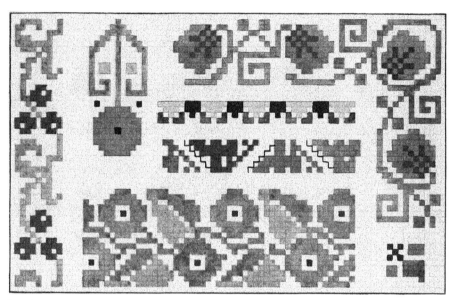

Page 18

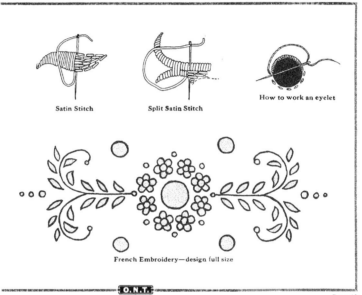

Satin Stitch   Split Satin Stitch   How to work an eyelet

French Embroidery—design full size

This design is given on page 19 in full size, and may be transferred by tracing first on transfer or tissue paper, and then pressing on the goods by means of a carbon paper. The design may be used for all kinds of fine lingerie, waists, children's dresses, aprons, etc.

O.N.T.

How to Launder Hand Embroidered Articles

Make a strong suds in a bowl or agate basin, being sure to use a pure white soap and water not too hot. Wash the piece or pieces of linen, rubbing the soiled parts between the hands; never rub soap on the embroidery. When clean, rinse thoroughly in several waters, and should the linen be at all yellow put some blueing in the final rinsing water. If it is too soft or slimsy dip in gum arabic water, but never use starch. Do not wring the linen, but instead partially dry by

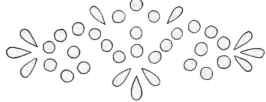

A French Embroidery Design

squeezing gently between two towels. Iron at once or, if this is not convenient, the linen may be rolled up in a towel and set aside for an hour.

The ironing board should be well padded or a large Turkish towel may be folded twice and laid over the board and the linen pressed on that. Lay it face down and cover with a damp cloth unless the linen itself is very damp, when the cloth may be used dry. Press from the center outward, first horizontally, with the grain of the goods, then perpendicularly. This prevents the centerpiece or doily from stretching or puckering out of shape. When the linen is almost dry the cloth may be removed, and the final pressing done on the wrong side of the centerpiece. Should it be impossible to get the linen to lie perfectly flat, try this method: While the centerpiece is still damp lay out smoothly on a well padded board. Pin the edge down firmly to the board, using fine steel pins so that the holes will not show when the pins are removed. Put the first pin in the center of one side, then place another directly opposite; next place one at the center top and bottom, then continue along the edge, taking care to keep the grain of the goods perfectly straight. Work in this way all around the edge of the centerpiece leaving it pinned on the board until thoroughly dry. This is an especially good method to follow for any centerpiece having a lace edge or for one that has been stretched out of shape by careless washing.

Smocking

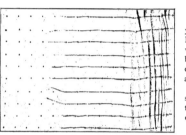

Smocking has gained wonderfully in popularity in the last year or so, particularly as a decoration for children's frocks. Most women have labored under the delusion that smocking was much too difficult for the home embroiderer to attempt, but this is far from being true. Anyone who can sew neatly, can quickly learn how to smock; it is merely a matter of neat and accurate stitchery.

The mother who makes her children's dresses will find smocking a decided factor in reducing their cost and adding to their charm, for with smocking as trimming lace and embroidery become superfluous.

Smocking can best be described as a form of ornamental shirring, the gathered material being worked over with colored threads to form a pattern. In order that the gathers may be perfectly even the material is first marked with a series of dots placed in even rows, at equal distances apart. Many of the prettiest patterns in smocking form points, and these may be made of any number of dots, providing that they are always divisible by four.

All smocking designs may be developed from the one foundation pattern, and if one plans to do much of this work, a perforated pattern of the rows of dots, with either powder or a paste and gasoline to transfer it to the material, is the most economical method to use. When only a little smocking is to be made the material may be marked off with the help of a ruler and lead pencil or a transfer pattern.

The following method, which does not call for the use of a dotted pattern, has been recommended by an expert in smocking: Thread the sewing machine with fine thread and use a coarse needle, very large stitch and a loose tension. Stitch as many rows as are necessary for the smocking, making them the width of the presser

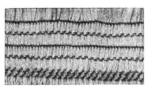

foot apart, by means of which it is a simple matter to keep the rows even. When the machine stitching is finished begin to gather, cutting the machine stitching at frequent intervals and pulling out the thread a little at a time, so that the row of holes will not be lost. A tiny stitch should be taken up at each hole and each line of gathering must have a separate thread. Begin each row at the right-hand side, fastening it firmly so that the knot cannot slip through. Let the end of the thread hang loose until all the rows have been gathered, then pull them up tight and fasten the ends of the various threads by winding them around pins, or by tying them together two and two, in a firm knot. When the smocking is finished the gathering threads should be pulled out.

This same woman also suggests that beginners may practice the various stitches on a piece of cross-barred dimity, running the gathering threads on the horizontal lines and taking up a stitch at each intersection. The quantity of material used in smocking varies greatly, according to the quality of the material and the size of the spaces between dots, but the English rule allows twelve inches of material for three inches of smocking.

It is next to impossible to say that any one thread is the best to use for smocking, for different materials require threads of different weight. Four or six strand cotton, a medium-weight marking cotton, O. N. T. "Lustre," and Pearl Cotton Nos. 5 and 8 are all suitable smocking threads, and the choice lies entirely with the worker.

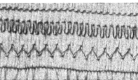

Just here it may be advisable to say a word as to the laundering of smocked garments. They may be washed and ironed the same as anything else, but afterward the smocked part should be placed face down on a Turkish towel and the edges pinned down to keep it flat. Dampen and iron crosswise until thoroughly dry.

The first illustration on page 22 shows how the gathering threads should be run in and also how the material should look when the gathering threads have been pulled up.

In the first detail on page 23 three different stitches are shown. The first row is outline stitch, the second single cable, the third another row of outlining, the fourth another single cable stitch, and the last a row of double cable stitch.

Outline stitch is used in starting nearly all patterns. It is worked from left to right, taking the stitches directly over the gathering thread and in this way keeping a perfectly straight line.

Start the thread on the second pleat on the wrong side of the material; put the needle through to the right side and take one stitch in every pleat, always keeping the thread *below* the needle.

Single cable is begun and worked just the same as outline stitch, with this exception—the thread alternates every stitch. In the first stitch the thread is below the needle and in the second stitch it is above the needle; for the third it is again below, and in the fourth above. This alternating of thread is carried on to the end of the row.

Double cable stitch, which is the last stitch in the first group, is—as its name implies—two rows of single cable worked close together. Work one row of single cable, keeping it a little above the gathering thread line, then work a second row a little below the gathering thread line. Be sure to reverse the stitches in this second row; that is, if the first row of single cable began with the thread below the needle, begin the second row with the thread above the needle and continue in this way all across.

The first stitch in the second illustration on page 23 is single cable, the second vandyke stitch, the third the first half of diamond stitch, and the fourth and last, plain outline. The first and last stitches have been described above, but both the vandyke and the diamond stitch are new.

O.N.T.

For the former work from right to left. Start the thread, as in outline stitch, bringing the needle up on the first pleat on the right side of material, half way between the first and second gathering thread; take a stitch through the first two pleats together, then take a second stitch to hold them firm. Next take a stitch over the second and third pleats on the line of the second gathering thread, fastening firmly with a second overstitch, same as before. Then return to the line of the first stitch—half way between the first and second gathering threads— and take the third and fourth pleats together, fastening with the overstitch. Continue working in this way to the end of the row. This stitch should always be started midway between two gathering threads and be worked down to the line, a space of half the distance between gathering threads separating all the rows.

Diamond stitch is worked from left to right. Bring the needle up in the first pleat on the right side of the material on the first gathering thread. Take a stitch in this first pleat with the thread below the needle, then one stitch in the second pleat beside the first stitch, with the thread above the needle; next come down to half way between the first and second gathering thread and take one stitch in the third pleat with the thread above and a stitch in the fourth pleat beside it with the thread below the needle. Then return to the line of the first and second stitches, taking a stitch in the fifth pleat with the thread below and in the sixth with the thread above. Continue working back and forth in this way until the line is completed, taking only one stitch in each pleat. The second half of the diamond is formed by starting on the second gathering thread and working up to half way between the first and second gathering, so that the stitches meet. The second half of the stitch is not shown in this illustration, but diamond stitch forms the lower part of the point in the first illustration on page 24.

In the second illustration on page 24 two decorative stitches which are sometimes used in combination with very elaborate smocking are shown. The first little leaf-like sprig is made with three bullion stitches forming each leaf and a row of outlining for the stems. Sprigs like these may be used as a finish for the ends of points or arranged to form a simple design on the plain material between bands of smocking.

The way to work the rosette or button shown in the center of the illustration is depicted just below, it being nothing more than a woven spider-web. Instead of carrying the weaving thread under and over the foundation threads, a back stitch is taken over every thread, thus making a raised effect. These little rosettes may be used on a smocked dress or blouse in place of buttons.

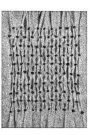

Honeycomb smocking, shown in the first illustration on this page, is worked from right to left. This is probably the simplest of the many smocking stitches. On ginghams or chambrays honeycomb stitch may be worked without the preliminary gathering threads, if desired, simply carrying the thread as close and firm as is possible between stitches without puckering the material. Begin by bringing the needle through to the right side of material at the second plait on the second line of gathering; draw the first and second plaits together with two over-and-over stitches, then go up to the third plait on the line of the first gathering thread, drawing the second and third plaits together in the same way. Return to the second line and take two stitches over the third and fourth plaits, being sure, in every instance, to carry the thread between the stitches on the wrong side; in this way nothing but the over-and-over stitches show on the right side. It will be apparent after half a dozen stitches have been worked that the last plait of one stitch is the first plait of the next stitch. Continue working in this way for as many rows as desired.

Wave stitch, shown in the second illustration on this same page, is somewhat more elaborate in effect, though very little more difficult to work. True, one must be very careful that no mistakes are made, no gathers skipped, for one error will throw the entire pattern out. Begin on the second plait on the wrong side, bringing your needle up in the first plait on the right side of the material. Take a stitch on the next plait, midway between the first and second gathering thread, then a stitch in the third plait on the second gathering thread, the next stitch on the fourth plait between the second and third gathering and the fifth stitch on the next plait on the line of the third gathering. On this down row always throw the thread below the needle. Next work back to the first row in the same way, taking each stitch on a separate plait but keeping the thread always above the needle.

The second and third rows are exactly the same, taking the first stitch in each row, one line below the preceding row.

If preferred, the rows may be worked much closer together by simply making the four stitches come between the first and second gathering threads. Wave stitch lends itself admirably to shading, a very pretty effect being gained if the upper rows are done in light shades, gradually letting the colors shade darker as the last row is reached.

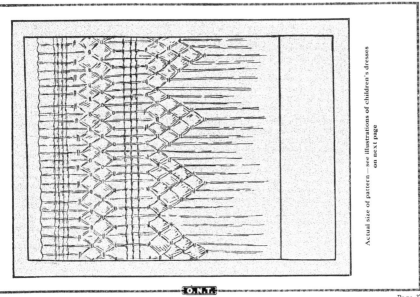

Actual size of pattern — see illustrations of children's dresses on next page

Showing how smocking may be used on children's frocks and rompers

O.N.T.

Flat-Stitch Embroidery

This work originated in Sweden and developed principally in the northern countries of Europe. Because of its highly decorative effect, other countries also accepted the flat stitch, and some of them introduced it even in their national embroideries, as, for instance, Hungary.

For anyone who has had some experience with the needle it is not difficult to work the flat stitch. It is carried out on the same plan as cross-stitch—in other words, the threads of the material have to be counted.

Naturally flat-stitch requires a material in which the threads can be readily counted. Scrim, coarse-woven linens and square-mesh nets, in either fine or coarse mesh, are the fabrics most desirable, and the patterns must be developed with rather a heavy thread in order to be effective.

Clark's O. N. T. Pearl Cotton in white may be used on the finer nets and scrim, being careful to choose the size best suited to the material. On the coarse scrim or loose-woven linen the embroidery may be worked in color if desired, carrying out the pattern in a single color or in a combination of shades which will harmonize with the general color scheme.

Unusually handsome bed spreads may be made of this flat embroidery, and when the material is not wide enough for the entire spread the widths may be joined by bands of hand-made Cluny or crocheted lace.

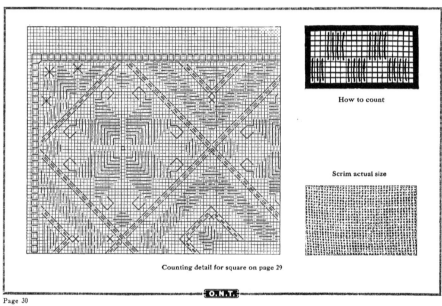

How to count

Scrim actual size

Counting detail for square on page 29

These flat-stitch designs can be easily followed and are very attractive for bureau or table scarfs

Swedish Weaving

Swedish weaving is a very attractive form of trimming for towels, table covers, scarfs, etc. It is particularly durable, for all of the drawn threads are covered in the weaving and the fancy border thus made is quite as strong as if the cross threads had not been pulled out. In making a towel it is advisable to choose a linen huckaback of good quality, for it is an extravagance to put so much work on poor material. For a full size towel one and one-quarter yards of huck twenty-seven inches wide will be required, while for a guest towel a yard of fifteen or sixteen inch huck will be sufficient; both of these measurements allow for hems. Baste the hems before drawing the threads for the weaving.

Before the weaving is started, baste the drawn portion of the material over a piece of green or black enamel cloth so that the weaving will not pucker or draw the linen out of shape. Use a needle with a blunt point and large eye, for a pointed needle will continually catch in the loose threads. Never make a knot but instead leave an end which can be covered and held firm by the weaving. Fasten this weaving thread by carrying it through the design already woven and by this means the work will be exactly alike on both the right and the wrong side.

Clark's O. N. T. Pearl Cotton should be used for the weaving, which may be done in either white or color. Be sure to select the size which is suitable for the damask or linen on which the work is to be done.

The patterns illustrated may be done in any desired width, but one must be careful not to have a wide border on a narrow towel. For a guest towel a border should be from three-quarters to one inch in width, while on a large towel it may increase from one and one-half to two inches. The same pattern should be worked on both ends of the towel, but should this entail too much work, one end may be finished with a plain or ladder hemstitch. Several attractive designs done in color are shown on page 17.

Bungalow Set

Solid Work

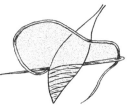

Modern embroidery is growing further and further away from the fine, careful work done in colored silks which was so popular some years ago. The needle-workers of today almost invariably demand a design which is conventional rather than floral in character, and one that will work in a quick, showy way.

The bungalow set illustrated in color on page 35 is an excellent example of the new style embroidery, and the colors used in developing the design are so soft and pleasing in coloring that they would harmonize with almost any surroundings.

In looking at the motif which is shown in full size on page 34, one might easily think that this design would entail considerable work, even though carried out with heavy thread. Such is not the case, however, when the stitchery used in developing the design is explained in detail.

Begin with the large center flower set at the top of the long, straight stem; this is worked solid, as are also the four leaves which grow below it. The two half flowers, set one at each side of the center, have solid center portions, but the backgrounds are seeded and the edges outlined. Next the buds are worked, making the little seed cups solid, the pointed flower parts in French knots and the small center part in seeding. All of the little round berries should be buttonholed, taking all of the stitches into the center hole, letting the back of the buttonholing finish the outer edge. Satin-stitch the leaves and work the jardiniere solid also.

The colors used in working out the design are given below:

Clark's O. N. T. Embroidery Cotton—Rope Size

Myrtle Green	No. 50	Deep Grape Purple	No. 60	Light Fawn	No. 97
Laurel Green	" 149	Light Yellow	" 2	Dark Brown	" 7
Light Blue Green	" 67	Light Maize Gold	" 18	China Blue	76
Pale Green	" 47	Pale Blue	91	Violet	44
Dark Willow Green	" 49	Cerise Pink	" 28	Mauve	40
		Black	White		

O.N.T.

BUNGALOW SET (See Page 33)

Cross-Stitch Embroidery

For linens, scrims and all evenly woven materials, cross-stitch embroidery is especially suitable as a mode of decoration, but it may also be worked on other fabrics quite as satisfactorily by means of a piece of rather coarse canvas, made especially for cross-stitch. This latter should be basted over the material and the cross-stitching done, taking the stitches through both canvas and material; when the design is completed pull out the canvas thread by thread. In cross-stitching a design where the canvas is used care must be taken that sufficient margin of plain canvas is left, at least at one side and at either the bottom or top, so that the threads may be readily pulled. Where the design is large the canvas threads may be snipped at intervals in order to pull out more easily.

Cross-stitch is so simple and easy to do that even small children soon learn to carry out simple designs of ducks, squirrels or children's figures, which are most attractive on towels or bibs. There is but one point to be emphasized and remembered: Always cross your stitches in the same way throughout the entire pattern. The detail figure shows clearly how this is done.

When worked on a loose-woven fabric cross-stitch may be done with a blunt-pointed, long-eyed needle, known as a tapestry needle, using O. N. T. Coton a Broder on O. N. T. 6 Strand Cotton. The color plate, page 18, gives a variety of motifs and borders which may be put to numerous uses, and any design made for filet or filet crochet may be carried out in cross-stitch, if desired.

An attractive cross-stitch motif

O.N.T.

Furnishings for a Bedroom

A simple rose design was chosen as the motif for this bedroom, and by a clever combination of attractive colors and simple stitchery an unusually artistic effect was obtained at a nominal cost.

A soft, rather loose-woven linen was used for the table cover, scarfs and pincushion, while the curtains, laundry bag and sofa pillow were made of scrim, of about the same color and weight. All of the embroidery was done with Clark's O. N. T. Embroidery Cotton, size Floria.

The rose motif is shown in actual size on page 39, while on the following page the same motif embroidered, and slightly enlarged, is pictured. By referring to the color plate, page 36, it will be seen that the motifs are joined by straight lines of outlining and the edges of both the pincushion and pillow are finished with a crocheted cord. Directions for making this cord will be found on page 47. The size used on the pillow requires three stitches, while the pincushion cord needs but two.

At the present writing bed spreads made of scrim are very popular, and deservedly so, for they are both inexpensive and easy to launder—two very desirable features in a bed spread. This rose motif would lend itself admirably for use on a spread whether made of plain or hemstitched scrim. Should the latter be selected, be sure that the squares formed by the hemstitching are large enough to hold the rose motif, then work a motif in every alternate square, leaving the intervening ones plain. Finish the edge of the cover with a hemstitched hem or with the chain braid to match the dresser scarf.

The roses should be done in No. 33 Rose Pink. For the round flowers use No. 91 Pale Blue and No. 44 Violet. The large leaves require No. 67 Light Blue Green, and the small dot in the center of the one little flower No. 18 Light Maize Gold. The outlines should be black, and the French knots No. 91 Pale Blue. For the eyelets on the laundry bag use No. 67 Light Blue Green, and make the cords with O. N. T. Pearl Cotton No. 1130 Dark Olive Green No. 5.

To make the border of the bureau cover, work a chain with the Pearl Cotton mentioned, and lay the chain wrong side up on the small hem around the cover. Then work it on with wide button-hole stitches, always going between the single stitches, which will appear as small pearls.

The method of attaching the chain is shown on page 39.

O.N.T.

The line cut on this page gives you the design for the bedroom set in the exact size. You can trace this design by using a small pointed stick or pencil, and tissue or real tracing paper.

Fasten (with two thumb tacks) on the material where the design is to be made, placing a sheet of carbon paper as large as pattern underneath the design, and trace carefully.

The design of the bedroom set in natural size

How to put the chain braid on the dresser scarf

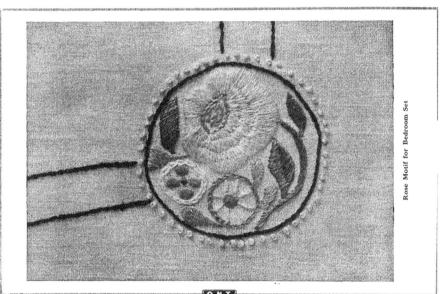

Rose Motif for Bedroom Set

O.N.T.

Crocheting

Table of Cotton and Hook Sizes

Clark's O. N. T. Crochet Cotton Nos.	1	3	5	10	15	20	25	30	40	50	60	70	80	100
Milward's Crochet Hooks Nos.	1	2	3	4	5	6	7	8	9	10	11	12	13	14

Abbreviations Used in Crocheting

st = stitch   sl st = slip stitch   dc = double crochet   p = picot   w st = wound stitch

ch = chain stitch   sc = single crochet   tr c = treble crochet   d = dot   m = meshes

★—Means to repeat directions printed between them as many times as stated in each case.

Crocheting is one of the most agreeable forms of fancy work and because of the simplicity of the four or five stitches which are most used, it presents but few difficulties to the beginner.

There is really but one stitch to learn—the chain; all the others are merely variations made by throwing or winding the thread around the needle a certain number of times and catching it into the work.

In working with cotton thread it is very desirable to learn to do work that is close, firm and even, for it is impossible to carry out a crochet design effectively if the stitchery is loose and uncertain. For this reason it is wise to do a little experimenting with the cotton and needle in the sizes suggested in the directions in order to determine that the needle really is the correct size for each individual worker. If one is inclined to crochet loose. it is advisable to select as fine a needle as can be used with the thread. while a comparatively coarse needle may be chosen if one's work is very tight. In buying a steel crochet hook be sure to select one that has a smooth; round head or hook, otherwise one is almost sure to have difficulty with thread that is pulled and split.

O.N.T.

Fig. 1

Chain Stitch (Fig. 1)—Chain stitch is the foundation of all crochet work. Begin by twisting the thread once around the hook to form a loop, then ★ catch thread around hook and draw through loop; this forms the first loop. Repeat from ★ for length desired.

Fig. 2

Slip Stitch (Fig. 2)—The slip stitch is used most often in joining rows together, or in going from one point to another invisibly, and sometimes for pattern effects.

Draw the working thread through the loop indicated in directions, or through chain made previously. Take thread over needle and draw with the same motion through loop. Only the upper threads of stitches of previous row are to be taken.

Single Crochet (Fig. 3)—Insert the hook in the foundation chain and draw thread through, catch thread around hook and draw through both loops on hook.

Double Crochet (Fig. 4)—Catch thread around hook, insert in chain, draw thread through; catch thread around hook, draw through two loops, thread around hook and draw through last two loops. Always start a d c row with 3 ch in place of the first dc.

Treble Crochet (Fig. 5)—The treble crochet is made similarly to the double crochet. Start with 4 ch and take thread twice over needle, drawing three times through two.

Fig. 3

Picot (Fig. 6)—Make a chain of three or four st as indicated in directions; throw cotton over hook, insert hook into first ch st made and make a single crochet.

Fig. 4

O.N.T.

Fig. 5

Crochet Dots (Fig. 7)—These dots, also called popcorn stitch, are made of double or treble crochet worked in groups. Instead of drawing the thread through the last time with each stitch, leave the loops on the needle, and draw through when you have made the number of doubles or trebles that the pattern demands.

Fig. 6

The Cross Double Crochet (Fig. 8)—This is a pretty stitch for beading on babies' apparel, lingerie, corset covers and various other articles on which an insertion for ribbon is desired.

Fasten thread in the work and start with 6 ch. ★ Take thread twice over the hook, skip 2 ch st of previous row, or leave a space accordingly. Draw thread through the loop. Thread over hook, draw through two; thread over hook, skip 2 ch, draw thread through third ch; thread over hook, draw through two; thread over hook, draw through two; thread over hook, draw through two.

Ch 2, thread over hook, insert needle taking up the two top threads of loop on crossing (see Fig. 8). Draw thread through and work off as a dc. Ch 2, skip 2 ch of previous row, and repeat from ★.

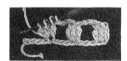

Fig. 7

Fig. 8

O.N.T.

Library Set
Made in the new O. N. T. Crochet Embroidery

Library Set in the New O. N. T. Crochet Embroidery

The library set illustrated on page 44 is made of golden brown burlap, with the crochet motifs and embroidery developed in green, brown and black. A Milward's Crochet Hook, No. 3, was used and Clark's O. N. T. Pearl Cotton, No. 3, large balls. The colors selected were 1130 Dark Olive Green, 1184 Russet, and Black, the combination being all that could be desired.

The Star of O. N. T. Crochet Embroidery—Take the green thread. Make a ch of 5 and close with sl st for a ring.

1st row—Ch 3, make a winding stitch with 5 windings (see Fig. 9) over the 3rd ch. Ch 3, ★ 1 dc in the ring of the 5th ch. A winding stitch around the dc (always take 5 windings for the whole star). Ch 3, repeat from ★ 4 times, having 6 winding stitches in all. Ch 3 and join with a sl st to the 3rd ch of commencement.

2nd row—Ch 3, 1 winding stitch over the ch of 3. ★ ch 3, 1 dc over the next 3 ch. A winding stitch around the dc. Ch 3, 1 dc on top of the winding stitch of previous row. 1 winding stitch over dc, repeat from ★ 4 times, ch 3 and fasten with a sl st on 3rd ch of the 1st row.

3rd row—Ch 6. 1 dc over the next 3 ch. Ch 3 ★ 1 dc on top of the next winding stitch. Ch 3, 1 dc over the next 3 ch. Ch 3 and repeat from ★ 9 times. Ch 3 and join as described before.

Use a coarse Milward Tapestry Needle No. 1, and fasten by sewing invisibly up and down through the crochet work.

A ch st row of black thread is sewed all around the star. Place the ch with the wrong side upward. After that the ch with winding stitch balls is embroidered around it.

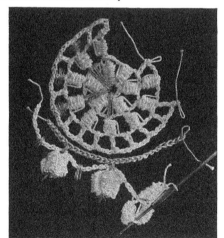

Chain with Balls in Winding Stitches—Ch 13 and ★ make a winding st (see Fig. 11, on page 47; always use 7 windings for the stitches) around the last 3 sc. Ch 3, a winding st over the 3rd ch. Ch 3, a winding stitch over the 3rd ch; fasten with a sl st on the 10th ch of ch of 13 made at the beginning. Ch 3 and make a winding st over the 3rd ch; fasten with a sl st on the bottom and between the two winding stitches made first, where no ch space is left between. Ch 3, make winding stitch and fasten in the 10th ch of the beginning. Ch 13 and continue from ★ until desired length of ball chain is accomplished.

Small Braid with Winding Stitch—A small braid with winding stitches is used for the border on the pillow, and it is also used for borders on dresser covers, etc.

Ch 6 ★ make a winding stitch with 5 windings around the last 3 ch stitches. Ch 6, repeat from ★ to desired length.

After laying the material flat on a table, place the stars and borders straight on the material. Baste the motif firmly in position, using the same thread as the piece is worked with threaded in a coarse Milward Tapestry Needle. After the motif is fitted, finish the embroidery stitches in black, as shown in the illustration.

Small Border Around Triangle Pillow (Fig. 10)—Take the green thread and ch 6.

1st row—1 dc in the 4th ch st, counting back 2 dc in the next ch. Ch 5, turn.

Fig. 9

2nd row—★ 1 dc in the third dc of previous row, ch 2, turn.

3rd row—2 dc over the last 2 ch of ch of 5 of 1st row. 1 dc in the 3rd ch of ch of 5 of 1st row. Ch 5, turn, repeat from ★ continuously.

Fig. 10

Cord Around Pillow (Fig. 9)—**1st row**—Ch 4 and join with a sl st.

2nd row—5 sc in this ring.

3rd row—1 sc in each sc of preceding row, picking up the inside thread.

4th row—1 sc in each sc, picking up from the outside of work the thread below the top row of sc. By working in the way described, the top meshes will turn inside and make the padding of cord. Continue same as fourth row until there is the length desired.

Winding Stitch—There is nothing prettier than the winding stitch made in Pearl Cotton. It may be worked with threads of varying weight, and used for borders on laces, for picot edgings and finishing of embroideries. First, make a foundation of either chain stitches or of double or treble crochet, as the pattern demands. Ch 3 stitches, ★ thread over needle, draw a loop underneath the ch st; thread over needle, draw loop again as described, and repeat from ★ 5 to 9 times, according to directions, then draw thread through all the loops at once. Do not work too tight or too loose. Hold the ch st with your left hand straight in working, and keep the hook of the needle downward.

Fig. 11

Two Pretty Crocheted Caps

The first cap is made in a most effective diamond pattern in double crochet and popcorn stitch. This latter is worked as follows: Work 7 dc under the ch, then put the hook through the top of the first dc and draw the loop through the stitch of the work and then through the stitch already on the needle; ch 1 to fasten. The abbreviation pc stands for popcorn stitch. The cap illustrated is made with O. N. T. Pearl Cotton No. 8 and is begun with a ch of 5 joined to form a ring.

1st row—24 dc in the ring, join with slip stitch.

2nd row—1 pc in first st, ch 2, skip 1, 1 dc, ch 2 ★; 1 pc in next st, ch 2, skip 1, dc in next st, ch 2; repeat from ★ around the row.

3rd row—1 pc on top of pc of previous row, ch 1, 1 dc in ch, 1 dc on dc, 1 dc in ch, ch 1 pc on pc, and repeat all around.

4th row—Pc on pc, ch 1, 1 dc under the ch, 1 dc on top of each dc of previous row and 1 dc under the ch, ch 1, pc on pc; repeat around the row.

5th to 10th rows—Same as 4th.

11th row—1 pc under the ch in front of the pc of the previous row, ch 2, 1 dc on the pc, ch 2, 1 pc under the ch. Ch 2, dc on 2nd dc and 1 dc on each dc following until within one st of the end (do not work the last stitch), ch 2, pc under the ch, ch 2, 1 dc on the pc, ch 2, pc under the ch, ch 2, beginning again at the 2nd st, dc in each st until within 1 st of the end, ch 2, pc under the ch, ch 2 and 1 dc on the pc, ch 2, 1 pc under the ch. Ch 2, skip 1 dc, put 1 dc on top of all except the last. Ch 2 and pc under the ch; repeat around until 7 sets of 2 pc are made. On the 8th ridge of pc make 1 pc on top of pc of the previous row, ch 2 dc on each dc, leaving off one at each end.

12th row—Pc on pc, ch 2, 1 dc under ch, ch 2, 1 dc under next ch, ch 2, pc on pc, ch 2, dc on each dc, except the first and last, pc on pc, ch 2, 1 dc on the ch, ch 2, 1 dc under next ch, ch 2, 1 dc under next ch, ch 2, pc in front, ch 2; repeat around the row.

13th to 15th rows—Same as 12th.

16th row—Same as 15th until six diamonds have been worked, then work 1 pc under ch in front of pc, 1 pc on top, and 1 pc in every other stitch until 3 pc's are made, 1 pc on pc, 3 across the top of the next diamond. 1 pc on pc, ch 2, dc under ch, ch 2 and dc under ch; repeat across diamond and pc on pc, ch 2, dc on each dc, dropping first and last, pc on pc, then meshes as before; repeat until the two diamonds that have the pc clear across are reached; these are left to form the back of the bonnet. Turn and work the 17th and 18th rows beginning and ending with the popcorn stitch to form the final border.

19th row—Pc in every other mesh. 1 ch between. **20th to 23rd rows**—Pc on pc and 1 ch between.

Edge front of cap with a row of shells made by placing 8 tr c on top of 1st pc, ch 2, 1 sc between first 2 pc's, ch 2, 8 tr c between 2nd and 3rd pc, ch 2, sc, ch 2; repeat across front and around back.

The second cap is made with O. N. T. Mercerized Crochet No. 10. Begin with ch 5, join; into ring put 2 sc, ch 2, 2 sc,

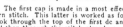

ch 2; repeat until there are 5 sets of 2 sc in the ring with 2 ch between the sets; ch 3, skip 1st sc and put 1 sc on the next sc, 2 sc under the ch of 2 st, ch 3, 1 sc over the second sc and 2 sc under the chain.

Rows 3 to 11 inclusive, same as second row. Always skip the first sc and always put 2 sc under the ch at the end, then ch 3 and repeat all around. There should be 14 sc in each cluster on this row.

12th row—After the 1st ch of 3 is fastened with a sc under the ch of 3 of the previous row, ch 3, and begin as before, skipping the first sc in each stitch across the section and 2 sc under ch; then, ch 3, and sc once under same chain; then ch 3 and skipping the first sc, work across as before; continue same way all around.

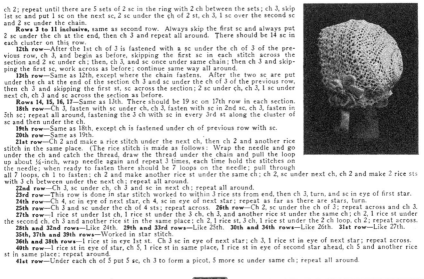

13th row—Same as 12th, except where the chain fastens. After the two sc are put under the ch at the end of the section ch 3 and sc under the ch of 3 of the previous row, then ch 3 and skipping the first st, sc across the section; 2 sc under ch, ch 3, 1 sc under next ch, ch 3 and sc across the section as before.

Rows 14, 15, 16, 17—Same as 13th. There should be 19 sc on 17th row in each section.

18th row—Ch 3, fasten with sc under ch, ch 3, fasten with sc in 2nd sc, ch 3, fasten in 5th sc; repeat all around, fastening the 3 ch with sc in every 3rd st along the cluster of sc and then under the ch.

19th row—Same as 18th, except ch is fastened under ch of previous row with sc.

20th row—Same as 19th.

21st row—Ch 2 and make a rice stitch under the next ch, then ch 2 and another rice stitch in the same place. (The rice stitch is made as follows: Wrap the needle and go under the ch and catch the thread, draw the thread under the chain and pull the loop up about ¼-inch, wrap needle again and repeat 3 times, each time hold the stitches on the needle; when ready to fasten there should be 7 loops on the needle; pull through all 7 loops, ch 1 to fasten; ch 2 and make another rice st under the same ch; ch 2, sc under next ch, ch 2 and make 2 rice sts with 3 ch between under the next ch; repeat all around.

22nd row—Ch 3, sc under ch, ch 3 and sc in next ch; repeat all around.

23rd row—This row is done in star stitch worked to within 3 rice sts from end, then ch 3, turn, and sc in eye of first star.

24th row—Ch 4, sc in eye of next star, ch 4, sc in eye of next star; repeat as far as there are stars, turn.

25th row—Ch 3 and sc under the ch of 4 sts; repeat across. **26th row**—Ch 2, sc under the ch of 3; repeat across and ch 3.

27th row—1 rice st under 1st ch, 1 rice st under the 3 ch, ch 3, and another rice st under the same ch; ch 2, 1 rice st under the second ch, ch 3 and another rice st in the same place; ch 2, 1 rice st, 3 ch, 1 rice st under the 2 ch loop, ch 2; repeat across.

28th, and 32nd rows—Like 24th. **29th and 33rd rows**—Like 25th. **30th and 34th rows**—Like 26th. **31st row**—Like 27th.

35th, 37th and 39th rows—Worked in star stitch.

36th and 38th rows—1 rice st in eye 1st st. Ch 3 sc in eye of next star; ch 3, 1 rice st in eye of next star; repeat across.

40th row—1 rice st in eye of star, ch 5, 1 rice st in same place, 1 rice st in eye of second star ahead, ch 5 and another rice st in same place; repeat around.

41st row—Under each ch of 5 put 5 sc, ch 3 to form a picot, 5 more sc under same ch; repeat all around.

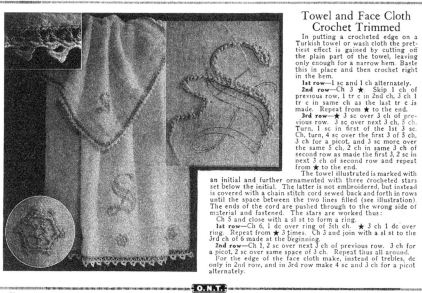

Towel and Face Cloth
Crochet Trimmed

In putting a crocheted edge on a Turkish towel or wash cloth the prettiest effect is gained by cutting off the plain part of the towel, leaving only enough for a narrow hem. Baste this in place and then crochet right in the hem.

1st row—1 sc and 1 ch alternately.

2nd row—Ch 3 ★. Skip 1 ch of previous row, 1 tr c in 2nd ch, 3 ch 1 tr c in same ch as the last tr c is made. Repeat from ★ to the end.

3rd row—★ 3 sc over 3 ch of previous row. 3 sc over next 3 ch, 5 ch. Turn, 1 sc in first of the 1st 3 sc. Ch, turn, 4 sc over the first 3 of 5 ch, 3 ch for a picot, and 3 sc more over the same 5 ch, 2 ch in same 3 ch of second row as made the first 3, 2 sc in next 3 ch of second row and repeat from ★ to the end.

The towel illustrated is marked with an initial and further ornamented with three crocheted stars set below the initial. The latter is not embroidered, but instead is covered with a chain stitch cord sewed back and forth in rows until the space between the two lines filled (see illustration). The ends of the cord are pushed through to the wrong side of material and fastened. The stars are worked thus:

Ch 5 and close with a sl st to form a ring.

1st row—Ch 6, 1 dc over ring of 5th ch. ★ 3 ch 1 dc over ring. Repeat from ★ 3 times. Ch 3 and join with a sl st to the 3rd ch of 6 made at the beginning.

2nd row—Ch 1, 2 sc over next 3 ch of previous row. 3 ch for a picot, 2 sc over same space of 3 ch. Repeat thus all around.

For the edge of the face cloth make, instead of trebles, dc only in 2nd row, and in 3rd row make 4 sc and 3 ch for a picot alternately.

Working Instructions for Sash Curtain Tulip Pattern

Materials: One ball O. N. T. 6 Cord Mercerized, No. 5, and a Milward's Crochet Hook, No. 4, is used.

Start with ch of 42, turn.

1st row—1 dc in 5th ch counting backward. 1 m (m represents mesh and consists of 2 ch and 1 dc after skipping 2 ch of previous row; this abbreviation is used in the following), 9 dc in the next 9 ch, 7 m. Ch 5, turn.

2nd row—1 dc in next dc of previous row. 12 dc, always over 2 ch and 1 on a dc. 1 m, 3 dc, 4 dc, 1 m. Ch 5, turn.

3rd row—1 dc on top of next dc, 3 dc, 4 m. 12 dc, 2 m. Ch 5, turn.

4th row—1 dc in next dc. 12 dc, 4 m, 3 dc, 1 m. Ch 5, turn.

5th row—1 dc in next dc, 5 ch, skip 2 ch and 3 dc of previous row, 1 dc in 4th dc, 9 dc, 6 m. Ch 5, turn.

6th row—1 dc in next dc, 4 m, 9 dc, 5 ch, 2 sc over center of 5th ch of previous row. 5 ch. 1 dc in next dc, 1 m. Ch 5, turn.

7th row—1 m, 5 ch, 2 sc over center of next 5 ch. 5 ch. Skip 3 dc of previous row, 9 dc, 1 m. Ch 5, turn.

8th row—1 dc in next dc, 2 m, 5 ch, 2 sc over next 5 ch. Ch 5, 2 sc over second 5 ch. Ch 3. 1 dc in next dc, 1 m. Ch 5, turn.

9th row—1 dc in 1st dc. Ch 5, 2 sc over next 5 ch. Ch 5, 3 dc over last 3 of chain of 5, 7 dc more over next meshes, 1 m. Ch 12, turn.

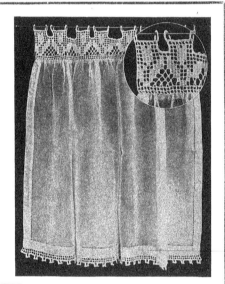

10th row—1 dc in 7th ch of ch of 12, counting backwards. 2 m over ch of 12, 2 m over previous row, 6 dc over next 6 dc, 3 dc over first 3 ch of 5 of row below., Ch 5, 2 ch over next ch of 5. Ch 5, 1 m. Ch 5, turn.

11th row—1 dc in next dc. Ch 5, 3 dc in last 3 ch of ch of 5. 7 dc over next 7 dc 6 m. Ch 5, turn.

12th row—1 dc over next dc, 12 dc over next 4 m, 2 m, 7 dc over next 7 dc, 3 dc, over next 3 dc of ch of 5, 2 m.

From instructions given the lace can easily be continued from the illustration. The bottom of lace is finished with one row, 2 ch, 1 dc, always following the end m of lace. Start the row with 5 dc.

The following is worked on the upper part, where the rod goes through the loops:

3 sc over next 3 ch, ch 12, fasten with a sl st in the first of 3 ch. Ch 1, make 20 sc, over ch of 12. ★ 3 sc in next 3 ch st of the m. Repeat from ★ 4 times, ch 12, join with a sl st in the 3rd last ch. Ch 1, 20 ch over ring of 12 ch, 3 more sc in the same m to build corner, and continue thus.

The small edge on bottom of the sash curtain is worked on a base of 15 ch. Turn, 1 dc in the 9th ch. Ch 2, skip 2 ch, 1 dc in the 3rd ch, 2 ch. Skip 2 ch, 1 dc in the 3rd ch.

2nd row—Ch 6, turn, 1 dc on top of next dc. Ch 2, 1 dc on top of next dc.

3rd row—The same as 2nd row.

4th row—The same as 3rd row. Ch 9, turn 1 dc in next dc, Skip 2 ch. Chain 2, 1 dc in next dc. Skip 2 ch, ch 2 ch, and repeat from 2nd row.

The outer edge is worked with 3 sc in each hole, and 1 p on each corner. This row is worked separately, after the lace is finished.

Towel End Trimmed with Motifs in Filet Crochet.
Made with 6 Cord Mercerized Crochet Cotton No. 30.

Working Detail of
Filet Motif

O.N.T.

Attractive Insertions in Filet Crochet

Mercerized Crochet Cotton No. 60 and a Milward Crochet Hook No. 13 are used for this exclusive pattern. Start with a ch of 52 stitches.

The design may easily be followed from the printed diagram. The filling of the squared places is done in the "Spider Filling," which is worked as follows:

1st row—1 dc. ★ skip 2 ch, 1 sc in next dc of previous row, 2 ch, skip 2 ch and make 1 dc over next dc of previous row. Repeat from ★.

2nd row—★ 1 dc in the dc of previous row, 4 ch, 1 dc in next row. Repeat from ★ continuously.

4th row—The same as 1st row, working the 2 rows alternately, but taking care that the ch bows all come in one line.

Any pattern of filet crochet lace can be worked with the spider filling. The mesh filling, however, may be worked right through if it is preferred.

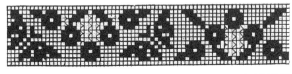

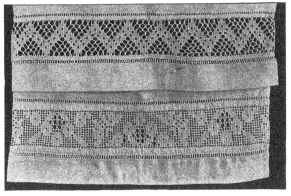

A Pretty Square Yoke in Crochet

Mercerized Crochet Cotton No. 70. Crochet Hook No. 9.

This crocheted yoke may be used in a chemise or corset cover and by changing the arrangement of the armholes it may also be set in a nightgown. The yoke is made in three pieces, the center band—an especially pretty fan pattern—being worked first, then the upper border, and finally the lower row of beading. Should it seem desirable to have a narrower yoke, this lower border may be omitted altogether and the fan insertion sewed directly on the undergarment.

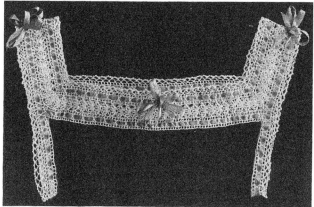

Crocheted Yoke for Chemise

1st row—Ch 4 and close with 1 sl st for a ring. Ch 4 again and make 1 tr c in ring of 4. ★ ch 2, 2 tr c in the ring, but do not draw thread through the last 2 loops of tr c but keep on needle and draw off with the first tr c. Work all pairs of tr c this way. Ch 4 and repeat three times, each pair of tr c being separated by 2 ch.

2nd row—Ch 4, 1 sc over the next 2 ch. Repeat this 4 times.

3rd row—Ch 6, turn, 2 tr c in the 3rd ch loop of 4 ch. Repeat from ★ to desired length.

Of this fan border work a piece long enough to go across the front and back and over each shoulder. Work this in one piece. The four corners, two in front and two in back, shape by gathering the ch a little and sewing the border in shape. Join the beginning and end of border by sewing invisibly. Continue with the outer borders, and when completed, join with a sl st and fasten threads.

The Top Border

For the top or the neck border, work on the side of the fan insertion, where the ch are made.

1st row—Ch 2, skip 2 ch of previous row and make 1 dc. Repeat this alternately.

2nd row—Ch 9, skip 2 st of previous row and make a cross dc catch over every next 2 ch.

3rd row—Ch, etc., same as 1st row.

4th row—★ ch 6, skip 1 ch space and work a sc over the second 2 ch. Repeat alternately from ★ to end.

5th row—3 sc over center of 1st loop of 6 ch, 3 p, 3 sc over next loop of 6 ch. Repeat from ★ to end.

To make the corners see detail illustration.

The Lower Border of Insertion

1st row—Join the thread in the first loop of 4 ch of fan with a sc, ★ ch 6, 1 sc in first loop of 4 ch of next fan. Repeat from ★ to the end of row.

The last rows are similar to the 1st row, 2nd row and 3rd row of top border.

For the lower part of sleeve under the arm, continue the top border all around sleeve according to the pattern used. See illustration.

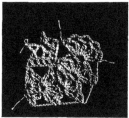

Corner-Detail of Crocheted Yoke

Filet Crochet Underwear Designs

Nightgown Yoke in Filet Crochet

This nightgown yoke, if intended for size 36, may be worked with No. 60 Mercerized Crochet Cotton on a scale of eight meshes to the inch; if intended for size 42, work with No. 40 Cotton on a scale of seven meshes to the inch. Changing the cotton and the size of the mesh in this way enables the needlewoman to make the yoke for any desired size.

Begin the yoke across one side of the lower edge of the front, with a chain of 48 stitches, working 45 double crochet across the chain.

Second row—Turn, chain 6, skip 3 chain, 1 double crochet in each of the others, 1 double crochet in each stitch across the row, and at the end add 3 chain stitches with an extra thread, on it working 3 double crochet. This row ends toward the center of the yoke. On it work according to the pattern until 16 rows have been made, and at the end of the sixteenth row chain 12 and fasten off.

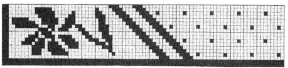

Detail of Half of Cuff to Match Yoke

O.N.T.

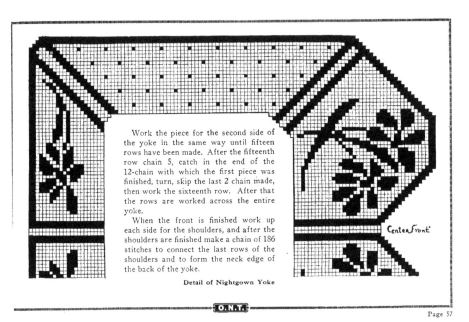

Work the piece for the second side of the yoke in the same way until fifteen rows have been made. After the fifteenth row chain 5, catch in the end of the 12-chain with which the first piece was finished, turn, skip the last 2 chain made, then work the sixteenth row. After that the rows are worked across the entire yoke.

When the front is finished work up each side for the shoulders, and after the shoulders are finished make a chain of 186 stitches to connect the last rows of the shoulders and to form the neck edge of the back of the yoke.

Detail of Nightgown Yoke

CenterFront

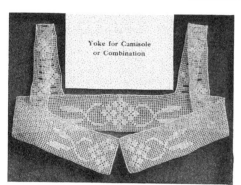

Yoke for Camisole
or Combination

When the yoke is finished, crochet around the neck edge as follows: Make 1 treble crochet in each of the first 4 stitches, chain 3, skip 3 stitches, and repeat around, joining at the end. On the outer edge work a row of holes, then on both neck and outer edges work a row of single crochet. After every fifteenth single crochet, chain 5, turn, catch in the third single crochet before the last one made, turn, in the new loop work 7 single crochet.

The band for the sleeve should be left open at the ends. The rows are worked crosswise, and the center part may be made as long as necessary for the width of the sleeve. Finish the ends and the outer edge with the same holes used for the outer edge of the yoke.

For the corset cover or camisole yoke use No. 60 Mercerized Crochet Cotton and do the work as nearly as possible on a scale of eight meshes to the inch. The rows should be worked up and down. Begin along the edge of one front with a chain of 68 stitches on which the first row of 21 holes should be worked; after that begin the design. After the design has been completed a sufficient number of plain rows should be worked, to make the strip long enough to reach from the center of the front to the center of the back, less 31 rows, upon which the first half of the design for the back is worked. Then make the second half like the first, finishing the top and end edges with single crochet.

If preferred the yoke may be closed all around, omitting the two center front rows of holes, and making it somewhat full, with the .fulness gathered on a ribbon run through the upper row of holes. Or the yoke may be closed in front and opened in the back by omitting the two center back figures.

Make the shoulder straps by working the first row in the proper position along the top edge of the strip for the yoke. Work the eyelets for the ribbon by omitting five holes in the row and making a chain of 14 stitches instead. When the strip is long enough, join it to the top of the back edge of the yoke, and fill the side edges with single crochet.

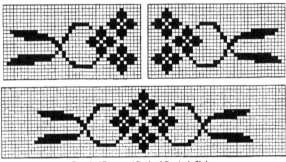

Detail of Front and Back of Camisole Yoke

In joining the crocheted yokes to the body of the nightgown or camisole it is wise to hem them down carefully to the nainsook or longcloth, first being sure that the fulness is properly adjusted. When this is done trim the surplus material away from the wrong side and roll and whip the raw edges, taking the stitches into the crocheting as well, thus making the joining doubly secure.

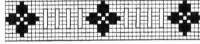

Detail of Shoulder Strap

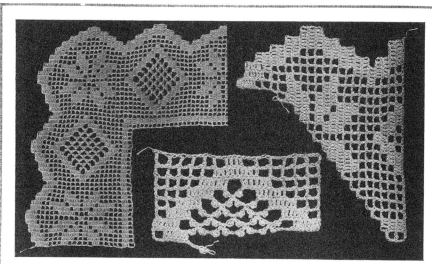

Crocheted Corner and Insertion

O.N.T.

Lace with Corner and Insertion

This lace is made with Mercerized Crochet No. 40 and Milward's Crochet Hook No. 11. The exact corner and the filling of the square are shown in the working detail. Make filet crochet, following the sketch as usual. 2 sc for the open and 4 dc for a solid square. This lace can also be made in Nos. 15 and 25 for bed spreads, sash curtains, table runners, etc., and in finer numbers, 60 and 80, it will be beautiful for centerpieces, fine towels, etc.

How To Make a Correct Corner in Filet Lace

When the point is reached on the straight side of lace where the corner begins, decrease the squares one in each row following. Turn thread 3 times around needle for a double treble, and work off. Ch 3, turn, and continue design (see illustration on page 60).

When making a zigzag ending with 4 dc, do not pull thread through the dc the second time, but make first all 3 dc half keeping the 5 loops on needle. Then work off, first through one and then two by two. Ch 2 and continue pattern. The zigzag line ends with 7 dc. Ch 3, turn, 3 dc in the next 3 dc. Ch 5, 1 dc in the second ch, 1 dc in the first ch, 3 dc in the side of last dc of last square made of zigzag line. Skip on the next corner of 2 ch, 1 dc, turn, 5 dc in the next 5 dc.

Ch 5, continue pattern to next corner, ch 2, skip on next corner. Ch 2, 1 dc in next corner, turn and continue pattern. Continue thus, finishing corner until the corners are all joined, and work the lace the usual way.

The picot filling in the squares after having accomplished the two first rows of the lace, work as follows: 7 dc for the 3rd row, 1 p, 1 ch, 1 p. Skip 2 dc and make 7 dc.

4th row—7 dc, 1 p, 1 ch, 1 p. Fasten in 1 ch between 2 p of previous row, 1 p, 1 ch, 1 p. Skip 3 dc of previous row, and make 7 dc as usual. Continue thus for two more rows.

7th row—7 dc as usual, 3 ch, 1 p. Fasten in 1 ch between 2 p and work thus 3 p bows, as usual. 1 p, 3 ch. Skip 3 dc of row below. 7 dc.

The 8th row will decrease the square and 3 dc are always to be made over the first and last 3 ch. Continue to end (see illustration on page 60).

Design Detail

Medallion in Irish Lace

Small squares of baby Irish lace like the one illustrated below are very easy to make and may be put to a number of different uses. They are especially effective in underwear, combined with a little French embroidery, and may also be used to good advantage on lingerie pillows.

Medallion Figure—Use O. N. T. Crochet & Tatting Cotton Nos. 30 to 80, and Crochet Hooks Nos. 8 to 14.

ROSE. 1st row—Ch 5 and join with sl st for a ring .

2nd row—Ch 6 (the first 3 counting as a dc after joining), 1 dc, 3 ch 5 times. Join with sl st.

3rd row—1 sc, 5 dc, 1 sc in each space. This will make 6 petals in all.

4th row—Ch 4. Fasten with sc on back of 2nd row between 2 petals. Ch 4, so between next 2 petals. Repeat around.

5th row—1 sc, 7 dc, 1 sc over each 4 ch of preceding row.

6th row—Ch 6, and proceed as in the 4th row.

7th row—1 sc, 9 dc, 1 sc in each 6 ch.

8th row—Sl st on third st in first petal.

For the beginning of the filling: Ch 6, catch back to third (for picot), ch 6, catch back to third, ch 3. This completes what is called a picot loop. Join with sl st to center of petal 1 picot loop, fasten in end of petal. Continue same over each petal, and join the twelfth one where the first one starts.

2nd row—Make sl st to center of next p loop in the back of stitches. Work picot loops all around to end of row. Fasten each loop with a sl st between the 2 p of each loop of previous row.

3rd row—Make 3 p loops. ★★ ch 6 and fasten in next loop as described above. Ch 3, turn, work 12 dc over the 6 ch. Ch 4, turn, ★ skip 1 dc of previous row, and make a dc in the second dc. Ch 1, repeat from ★ to ★ to end of dc. Work a p loop, fasten with sc at the same place where the 6 ch are fastened. Make 2 more p loops, and repeat from ★★.

4th, 6th and 8th rows are like the second row. Over the dc make 2 p loops.

5th and 7th rows are like the 3rd row.

O.N.T.

Venetian Crochet Insertion

This insertion is adaptable for bed linen as well as for towels, table linen and many other purposes. It is worked in Six Cord Mercerized Crochet Cotton No. 30.

The figures first have to be worked separately on a basis of 3 ch closed for a ring. Ch 6, 1 tr c in the ring of 3, ch 3, ★ 1 dc in the ring of 3, ch 3 and 1 tr c in ring of 3, ch 3. Repeat from ★ twice. Ch 3 and join to the 3 ch of start of 6 ch. Now work in each ch 1 sc all around the square, working in each tr c and in the 3 ch of start of 6, 3 sc to form the corners.

Work sc over the next side of square. Form the first pyramid by decreasing at end of each row 1 st and working forward and backward with sc, taking only the back loops of stitches, until 1 sc is left. Work with sl st down on left side of triangle to the square again. Make the next 3 pyramids the same way, cutting off thread and fastening. It is advisable first to make enough of these figures and small squares for the length of insertion desired.

The small squares are made by making a ch of 10 and working 10 rows of sc, taking only the back loops.

After all the figures are finished join the thread in the corner of one pyramid. ★ ch 12, 1 double treble—that is, the thread taken 3 times around needle in the corner of square between lower part of pyramids. Ch 7, 1 dc in top of the double treble, ch 4, 1 sc in top of next pyramid. Repeat from ★ all around, and join on the end. Now crochet over the chain without counting, putting the sc close together. The corners are formed by working 3 sc into the center or corner sc of preceding row. On two sides work 5 dc rows, going forward and backward.

Sew the little squares as shown in picture between the sides of 5 dc rows.

After all the lengths of lace are joined, work the top and bottom rows. Join on one corner of a large square, where one sc row starts. ★ Make 1 dc in each st of previous row until the 5th row of the 5 sc row is reached. Ch 8, 1 tr c in corner of small square, ch 3, turn, 1 dc in 4th ch of 8, ch 6, 1 tr c in corner of small square. Ch 3, turn, 1 dc in 3rd ch of 6, 1 sc in corner sc of next large square. Repeat from ★ to end of row, and repeat the row also for the other side of insertion.

The two side edges are worked as follows: Ch 6 to start with, after having joined thread at the beginning of insertion. ★ Skip 3 sc, 1 sc in the 3rd sc. Ch 1, turn, 4 sc over the next 3 ch of ch of 6. Ch 6, and repeat thus from ★ for both sides of insertion to the ends.

The upper ch rows are finished off on both sides with a row of sc, making 4 in each ch space.

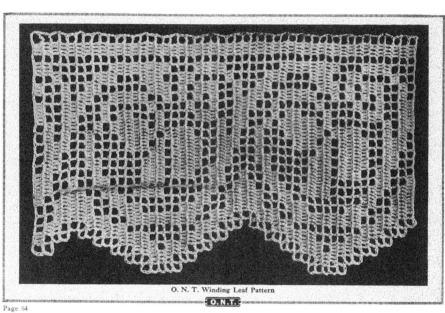

O. N. T. Winding Leaf Pattern

O.N.T.

Making Crocheted Doily

Ch 5 and close with a sl st for a ring.

1st row—1 sc and 2 ch st alternately 10 times in the ring of 5 ch. Repeat this row 10 times, making the sc always over the 2 ch of previous row. Increase on every 5th sc by making 2 more sc; this widening makes the work lie flat.

12th row—Ch 4, 1 dc over the next 2 ch of previous row. ★ 1 ch, 1 dc over next 2 ch, 1 ch, 1 dc in same 2 dc. Repeat from ★ all around and close row with sl st taken in to 3 ch made at beginning.

13th row—Ch 4, 3 tr c over next 1 ch of previous row. The trebles are joined on top by slipping off together. ★ ch 4, skip 1 space of 1 ch and make 4 tr c in next space of 1 ch; repeat from ★ all around. End with 4 ch and join with a sl st.

14th row—Ch 4, 1 dc, 1 ch alternately 3 times, catching in each ch of previous row, and 3 times skip 1 ch of previous row. Repeat this all around, ending with 1 ch and joining with a sl st.

15th row—9 ch, 1 tr c in the second dc of previous row. ★ ch 5, 1 tr c in 2nd dc; repeat from ★ ending with 5 ch and join with sl st to the 4th st of first 9 ch.

16th row—Ch 4, ★ 1 dc in 2nd ch of previous row, ch 1; repeat from ★ all around and join.

17th row—Ch 4, 3 tr c over next ch of previous row, joined as described in 13th row. 3 ch, 1 sc on top of 3 tr c. Ch 6, ★ skip 2 spaces of previous row, 4 tr c in 3rd space, 3 ch. 1 sc in top of 4 tr c; ch 6 and repeat from ★ all around. Join when finished.

18th row—Catch with a sl st in the 1st 3 ch loop on top of 3 tr c. Ch 4, 3 joined tr c in same loop. ★ Ch 8, 4 more joined tr c in same loop, 4 joined tr c in next loop on top of next 4 tr c of previous row. Repeat from ★ all around and join.

19th row—In each of the next 4 ch make 1 sl st. Ch 4, 3 joined tr c in first 8 ch loop of previous row. ★ Ch 8, 4 joined tr c in next 8 ch loop; repeat from ★ all around, 8 ch and join.

20th row—Ch 4. ★ Skip 1 ch of previous row, 1 dc in next ch, ch 1; repeat from ★ all around.

21st row—Work the same as 15th row.

22nd row—The same as 16th row.

23rd row—Ch 4, 3 joined tr c over next ch of previous row. ★ Ch 5, skip 2 spaces and make 4 joined tr c in 3rd space. . Repeat from ★ and join.

24th row—Ch 4. ★ 5 times 2 ch and 1 dc in each 3rd ch of previous row. Ch 6, turn. 1 sc in the next 2ud dc. Turn, ch 3 for a p, 1 dc in the loop of 5 ch 4 times, 1 p, 1 dc in same loop, 1 dc in 3rd ch of 22nd row. Repeat from ★ all around.

Cut off thread and fasten invisibly.

O.N.T.

Filet Crochet Design for Lower Edge of Curtain

The Laundry Bag

The laundry bag which is illustrated on page 69 is made of a medium-weight ecru linen and trimmed with a crocheted lace made with Clark's O. N. T. Crochet Twist, Ecru No. 5. This crochet twist is made in ecru, linen and Arabian, as well as white, so that it would be a comparatively simple matter to carry out the same design in a color which would match the furnishings of the room in which it is to be used. The edges of the linen are finished with a hemstitched hem about an inch wide and the crocheted banding is then whipped firmly to the double edge of the material. If desired, a crocheted cord, similar to the one illustrated on page 47, may be worked and used in place of the ribbon hanger. The bag is 15 inches wide and 36 inches long, finished. The short end will be found convenient for handkerchiefs, collars and fine lingerie, while larger garments may be placed in the long end of the bag.

Materials, Clark's O. N. T. Crochet Twist No. 5. Milward's Crochet Needle No. 4.

DIRECTIONS: Start with a ch of 40.

1st row—Turn the work. Skip 9 ch, counting back, and make 1 dc in the 10th ch. Ch 2, 1 dc in the same loop as the one made before. Skip 1 ch, 1 dc in the 2nd ch. Ch 2, 1 dc in the same ch. Skip 1 ch, Ch 1, 1 dc in the 2nd ch. Ch 2, 1 dc in the same loop. Ch 4, skip 3 ch, 1 dc in the 4th ch. Ch 2, 1 dc in the same loop. Ch 5, skip 4,

1 tr c in the 5th ch. Ch 5, skip 4, 1 dc in the 5th ch. Ch 2, 1 dc in the same loop. Ch 4, skip 3, 1 dc in the 4th ch. Ch 2, 1 dc in the same. Ch 1, skip 1 ch, 1 dc in the 2nd ch. Skip 1, 1 dc in the same loop. Ch 2, 1 dc in the last loop of row. Ch 5 and turn.

2nd row—1 dc over the next 2 ch between the 2 dc of previous row. Ch 2, 1 dc over the same ch. 1 dc over the next 2 ch. Ch 2, 1 dc over the same ch. Ch 4, 1 dc in center of the next 4 dc of previous row. Ch 2, 1 dc over same space. Ch 4, 3 dc in the last 3 ch of 1st ch of 5 of previous row, 1 dc in the top of the tr c, 3 dc over the next 3 ch. Ch 4, 1 dc in center of next 4 ch. Ch 2, 1 dc in same space. Ch 4, then repeat the border as described before and continue it on both sides. The directions are mentioned further from 1 to the last dc of border.

3rd row—Border, ch 2, 1 dc, 1 ch and 1 dc over the center of next 4 ch. Ch 4, 3 dc in the last 3 ch, next ch of 4 ch, 7 dc in the next 7 dc and 3 dc in the next 3 ch. Ch 4, 1 dc in center of next 4 ch. Ch 2, 1 dc in same space, ch 2, border.

4th row—The same as 2ud row.

5th row—The same as the 1st row, only worked according to pattern. Commence from 2ud row again, and continue the rows thus until the desired length is obtained.

O.N.T.

A Handsome Laundry Bag

Crocheted Cap and Jacket For a Baby

Size from 1 to 6 Months

MATERIALS REQUIRED FOR JACKET—4 Large Balls or 8 Small Balls Clark's O. N. T. 4 Strand Cotton, 1 Medium Ball Clark's O. N. T. Pearl Cotton, No. 5. Color as Desired.

The best results will be obtained if the work is done with a fine bone needle.

The shaping of the jacket is very simple, as it is put together with 5 straight, square pieces.

Start with the back and ch 73, turn, and work back in each ch 1 dc.

First shell stitch row—Ch 3, turn, 4 dc in 4th ch counted back. ★ skip 1 dc of previous row. 1 sc in second dc. Skip the third dc and make 5 dc in fourth dc. Now repeat from ★ to end of row.

Second shell stitch row—Ch 3, turn, 2 dc in last sc of previous row. 1 sc in 3rd dc of previous row. ★ 5 dc in next sc. Repeat from ★. 1 sc in 3rd dc of next shell. Repeat thus from ★ sh st to end of row. End row with 3 dc, and start next row with 5 dc.

Finish thus the back for 8-inch length. Then cut off thread long enough to thread in an embroidery needle, and fasten by sewing invisibly through the crochet. For the two front pieces ch a foundation of 40 loops, and work just like the back—8 inches long. Ch 50 for the two sleeves. Work like the other pieces, making them 6 inches long. When all pieces are finished, lay the front pieces on top of the back piece, sewing them together on the wrong side 4 inches from the bottom with invisible overcasting stitches. The upper open parts are the armholes. For the shoulder part sew two and one-half inches of the last shell stitch rows together.

O.N.T.

Now sew together the sides of the two sleeve pieces, and insert sleeves in the armholes. Then proceed with the border around the jacket and for the neck.

Join the colored Pearl Cotton in bottom corner. Ch 3, 1 dc in next ch of start. ★ skip 2 ch, make 2 ch and work 2 dc in next 2 ch. Repeat from ★ to end of row. Cut off thread and fasten.

Join white 4 Strand thread. Ch 3, 1 dc in each st of previous row to end of row. When last dc is made ch 9. Turn around front corner and continue with 2 ch, skip 1 dc and make 1 dc in side of crochet. Ch 2 and continue the same along side of front piece up to the neck. Ch 3, 1 dc in same space where last dc is made. Turn around for neck. ★ 3 dc in next 3 st. Do not pull thread through twice, but leave last 2 loops on needle until there are 6 loops. Pull through at once and repeat from ★ all around neck. This row will narrow the neck to fit.

Now work down the other side of front and work along the bottom until the beginning of row of 9 ch. End with 2 ch and join with a sl st to the 3rd ch of beginning. Cut off thread and fasten.

Join the colored Pearl Cotton over the 6 ch left from start. Ch 3, 1 dc in same space, ch 1, 2 dc in same space, ch 1, 2 dc in same space, 1 ch and 2 dc over each next space. Crochet loosely all around jacket. When all around, join to 3rd ch from start. Work 6 dc and 2 ch in one corner space of neck and bottom corner as described. Cut thread and fasten.

Join the 4 Strand thread in first 2 ch of bottom corner. Ch 1, 2 dc in next space of 2 ch. ★ 1 p (p, that is, ch 3, 1 sc in first of 3 ch) 2 dc in same space, 1 sc over next 1 ch, 2 dc over next 2 ch. Repeat from ★ to end of front. For the neck, instead of a p, make 2 ch only to end of neck. Ch 3, turn, go back on neck row the same way as last row made. Turn, make a p again and work back once more, but the third time make the p between the 4 dc all along the row. Now work down the other front side, and join on the bottom as described. Cut thread and fasten. Work all the border rows of bottom of jacket around the sleeves.

This jacket may also be worked of Pearl Cotton No. 5 only.

MATERIALS REQUIRED FOR CAP—2 Large Balls or 4 Small Balls Clark's O. N.T. 4 Strand Cotton, 1 Medium Ball Clark's O. N. T. Pearl Cotton No. 5, in Desired Color.

Ch 4 and close with a sl st for a ring.

1st row—Ch 3, 14 dc in ring of 4 ch. Join with sl st to 3rd ch of start.

2nd row—Ch 5. ★ 1 dc in next dc of previous row, ch 1 and repeat from ★ all around. Join as described.

3rd row—Ch 3, 2 dc over next ch, 1 dc in next dc. Leave the white 4 Strand thread hanging, and join the colored Pearl Cotton.

4th row—Ch 4. ★ 1 dc in next dc, ch 1, repeat all around and join. Cut off thread and fasten as described.

5th row—Ch. 3 with the white 4 Strand, 1 dc over next 1 ch, 2 dc in next 2 ch. Repeat all around and join. From 6th to 11th row inclusive, make a sh st. See the description.

12th row—Work sh st until 4 sh st are left; then turn and make sh st back. Work sh st from 13th to 21st row going forward and backward, thus building the front part of cap.

Border of Cap: 1st row—Ch 3, skip 1 st of previous row and make 1 ch, 1 dc in 2nd st of previous row. Work thus until corner and form corner by making 3 dc in one space alternately with 1 ch. When all around cap, join as usual. Cut thread, fasten, and join the colored Pearl Cotton.

2nd row—Start with 3 ch, 1 dc over next ch. Ch 1, 2 dc over next ch, continue all around. Work in corners 4 dc separated by 2 ch. When all around join and cut thread. Join 4 Strand thread.

3rd row—Ch 6, skip 2 dc, ch 2, 1 dc over 1 ch of previous row. On end of row join as described. Ch 3.

4th to 9th rows, inclusive, are to be worked only on the front part of cap.

4th row—1 dc in each st of previous row. On end of row ch 6 and turn.

5th row—Skip 2 dc of previous row, ch 2, 1 dc in 3rd dc.

6th row—The same as the 4th row.

7th row—The same as the 5th row. Cut thread and fasten.

8th row—Join the colored Pearl Cotton. Ch 3, 1 dc over next 2 ch. Ch 1, 2 dc over next 2 ch of previous row. On end of row cut thread and fasten.

Join the 4 Strand thread. Ch 5.

9th row—I dc over next ch of previous row. Ch 2, 1 dc over next ch. Continue to end of row.

10th row—To work all around, turn half to neck part of cap and work over side of front part; 2 dc over the next colored dc, 1 p, 2 dc over same dc, 1 sc over next white dc, 2 dc over next dc, 1 p, 2 dc over same dc, 1 sc over next dc, 4 dc and 1 p over next dc, 1 sc over next 5 ch. ★ 4 dc, 1 p over next 2 ch, 1 sc over next 2 ch. Continue from ★ all around cap. Work the other side of border according to description for first side. Join, cut thread and fasten as described in beginning of description.

This cap may also be worked with Pearl Cotton No. 5 only.

Narrow Crocheted Edgings for Children's Lingerie

No other kind of lace is so durable as that which is hand crocheted, and for that reason no other lace is so entirely satisfactory for use on children's clothes. Many busy mothers feel that it is a waste of time to make elaborate insertions and edges to use on little garments which have to withstand such

No. 1

constant wear and tear, but narrow edges, such as are illustrated on this page, may be worked up so rapidly that this objection does not hold good.

Any one of these edges may be used to good advantage, not only on underwear and frocks for little children, but also on babies caps, pique coats, lingerie pillows and pique carriage covers. .

The size of the thread to be used for the work must depend, to a great extent, on the material on which it is to be used, for a much finer thread must be chosen for lace to go on a batiste or linen dress than on an edge which is to finish a garment made of pique.

A most attractive insertion and edge to match are shown in the last illustration on page 74. Begin with a chain of 15 and join the last and first st by a sl st. Ch 3, ★ turn, make 16 dc in ring of 15 ch. Ch 1, turn work. 2 sc in the next 2 dc of previous row. Ch 3, join with sc in the first ch for a p. Continue with sc to end of row. Ch 1, turn, 2 sc in next 3 sc, 1 p as described before, 3 sc in next 3 sc, 1 p and 3 sc. Ch 9, turn, fasten in the middle sc between the two p with sc, ch 3 and begin from ★ again. Continue working these fan figures one after the other until the desired length is completed, after which the little chain border may be started.

No. 2

Ch 10 and fasten in one corner of next fan. Ch 7 and fasten in corner of next fan. Work this all around the border, making on the point of each corner 8 to 10 ch and 3 sc in the 3 center stitches of fan, thus forming the edge.

For the last row ch 4, skip 1 ch, 1 dc in 2nd ch. ★ Ch 1, 1 dc, repeat from ★ all around insertion. For the corners work twice 2 dc in one ch. When

No. 3

all around join the last ch .to the 3rd of first 3 ch made with sl st. Cut off thread and fasten by sewing invisibly with a sewing needle.

For the Edge—Ch 12 and join with 1 sl st to a ring. ★ Ch 3, turn, make 9 dc in the ring of 12; ch 1, work 1 sc in each dc. Ch 1, turn, make 2 sc in next 2 sc. Ch 3 and join for a p as described in insertion. 3 sc in next 3 sc, 1 p, 3 sc in next 3 sc. Ch 9, turn, and continue from ★ for length desired.

When finished, ch 5. ★ 1 dc in side of next sc. Ch 1, 1 dc in center of side of next dc. Ch 1, skip 1 ch, 1 dc in next ch. Ch 1, skip 1 ch, 1 dc in next ch. Repeat from ★ to the end. Cut off thread and fasten.

For the little edge shown in the first illustration on page 73, start with a ch of 9 and turn.

1st row—Counting back, make a dc in the 5th ch, skip 2 ch, and make a dc with 2 ch between in the 3rd ch.

2nd row—★ Ch 5, turn, one dc over the next 2 ch of previous row, 2 dc with 2 ch between over the next 2 ch. Ch 3, 1 sc over the 3 ch left of first row. 1 ch, turn.

3rd row—3 times 2 sc alternately with 2 ch for a p over the next 3 ch.

4th row—Ch 5, one dc over the next 2 ch of previous row. 2 dc with 2 ch between over the next 2 ch. Repeat from ★ to desired length.

Begin the little pointed edge pictured in the second illustration on page 73 with 11 chain and turn.

1st row—★ 1 sc in the 2nd ch counted backwards. 3 dc in the next 3 ch, skip 2 ch of start, ch 2, 1 dc in 3rd ch. Skip 2 ch, ch 2, 1 dc in 3rd ch.

2nd row—Ch 5, turn, 1 dc in next dc of previous row. Ch 2, 1 dc in next dc of previous row, ch 5, turn and repeat from ★ to desired length.

The third design illustrated above combines a beading with the little scallop and is begun with 12 ch, turn.

1st row—Counting back, make 2 dc over the 7th and 8th ch of previous row. Ch 2, skip 2 ch of previous row and make 1 dc in first st made.

2nd row—Ch 5, turn, 2 dc over the next 2 dc. Ch 2, 1 dc in 3rd next ch.

3rd row—Ch 5, turn, 2 dc over next 2 dc. Ch 2, 1 dc in 3rd ch, 4 times 2 ch and 1 dc over next 3 ch on side of next mesh. For the scallop, ch 2, 1 sc in the following mesh. ★ 3 ch, turn, 1 sc over next 2 ch. Repeat from ★ 4 times. Ch 3, 1 dc in next dc. Ch 2, 2 dc in next 2 dc, ch 2, 1 dc in 3rd ch of turn. Repeat from 2nd row to length desired.

No. 4

O.N.T.

Tatting

Tatting is a kind of lace-work made with a shuttle which originated probably from a desire to reproduce the gimp or knotted laces of the sixteenth century by a simpler and easier method.

In the eighteenth century, when the vogue of tatting was at its height, it was used not only on clothes and household linens, but also as a finish for upholstery or curtains, in place of gimp.

The best material to use for tatting is Clark's O. N. T. Crochet & Tatting Cotton, as it is just sufficiently twisted for making a nice, smooth braid. As tatting is often finished off with a few rows of crochet, or crochet put in the middle of insertion, it is well to use a size coarser for the crochet than for tatting. Thus: if No. 80 were used for the tatting, No. 70 should be chosen for the crochet. O. N. T. Crochet & Tatting Cotton comes in six sizes, 30 to 80. Clark's O. N. T. Six Cord Mercerized Crochet Cotton can also be used with splendid results. This is obtainable in fourteen sizes, 1 to 100. For curtains and hangings tatting is an effective edging when worked with coarser thread.

Tatting shuttles are made of two double-pointed oval blades of a hard substance, such as bone, mother of pearl, tortoise-shell or hard wood. The shape of the shuttle is quite important for quick and perfect execution of this work. It should not be more than 2¾ inches long and ¾ inch wide. With two-shuttle work you must be sure that the blades are sufficiently close together at the end to prevent the thread from slipping out too quickly.

Fig. 1

The hole in the center piece between the blades should be large enough to admit and hold the thread for winding on the shuttles. Do not wind too much thread on the shuttle, else the blades will gape apart and thus be awkward to use.

For rings only one shuttle is necessary, but for scallops two shuttles are employed.

The drawings give you the position of the hands and the working of the shuttles.

Fig. 2

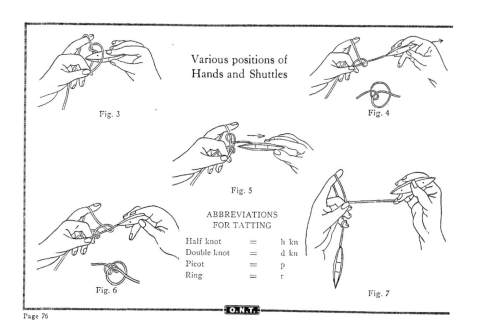

Various positions of
Hands and Shuttles

Fig. 3

Fig. 4

Fig. 5

ABBREVIATIONS
FOR TATTING

Half knot	=	h kn
Double knot	=	d kn
Picot	=	p
Ring	=	r

Fig. 6

Fig. 7

Directions for Tatting

First of all, try to remember from the very beginning that the right hand, as soon as the shuttle has passed the loop, should stay in position, motionless.

After winding sufficient thread on shuttle, take the end of the thread in left hand, between thumb and forefiuger. Take shuttle in right hand and hold the thread over the third and fourth fingers of left hand, bringing it back to the thumb, crossing the threads under the fiuger (see Figs. 1, 2 and 3, on pages 75 and 76).

Pass the shuttle between the first and third fingers, and bring it out behind the loop (Fig. 2, page 75).

Now comes the only trick in tatting. As soon as you have passed the loop with shuttle, give a quick jerk with the first finger of left hand, leaving the thread sufficiently loose over the same finger, that it may twist to a knot, and thus build the loop with the thread on left hand. Do not move the right hand, and hold the thread tight. The right hand may be resting on the table (Fig. 4).

When the loop is made, it is the first part of the double knot, a half knot. The second part of the loop is formed as follows: Pass shuttle from left to right between the first and third fingers through the extended loop. Fig. 5 shows the first motion before the jerk. Fig. 6 shows the position of threads after the jerk. The right hand seizes the shuttle in front of the empty loop and extends the thread. Now jerk the thread for the loop the same way as you did in the first part of the knot.

It is well to practice making this knot until one can do it perfectly before starting any work.

If the thread in the ring will not pull, making the ring smaller or larger, the manipulation is wrong.

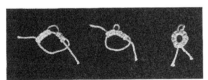

Fig. 1

Fig. 2

Tatted Lace for Centerpiece

This lace may be done in Nos. 15-80 of 6 Cord Mercerized Crochet Cotton, according to the quality of cloth to be used. It is designed especially for luncheon sets or centerpieces. The center design of lace is to be worked first.

Knot 2 shuttles together, and start with one for a ring.

★ r. 4 d kn, 1 p, twice 3 d kn, 1 p. End with 4 d kn and close ring. This is the ring used for the whole center design, and the description will not be repeated.

Take up the other shuttle and turn the work. Work a bow of 3 d kn, 1 p, repeat twice and make 3 d kn. Turn work and make a ring. Join the first p with the last p of last ring made. Repeat now from ★.

This repeated three more times will accomplish the first scallop of the center design. Now start for another bow from first ★ over again and join the first and second p of next bow with the second and third p of last bow. Then finish first bow as usual, and continue to the desired length of lace.

Inner Edge of the Lace—Work with two shuttles, and fasten them on first p of first ring. Begin with a bow of two shuttles. 5 d kn, 1 p, 5 d kn. This will be the bow for the inner edge and the description will not be repeated.

Turn the work and make a ring. ★ 3 d kn, join in top p of next ring. Repeat from ★ four times and close ring with 3 d kn. Turn the work and make a bow with 2 shuttles. Fasten in p of next ring, make another bow and fasten in first p of next ring. Repeat from first ★ continuously until end of lace.

Lower Scalloped Edge of Lace—Fasten 2 shuttles in the p left on first bow. ★ 2 d kn, 1 p, 2 d kn. Join in the second p of next bow. 2 d kn, 1 p, 2 d kn, 1 p, 2 d kn. Turn work and make a ring. 2 d kn, join in last p of next bow of previous row, 2 d kn, 1 p, 2 d kn, 1 p, 2 d kn, turn work and take up second shuttle for a bow of 2 d kn, 1 p, 2 d kn, 1 p, 2 d kn, 1 p, 2 d kn. Turn work for a ring, 2 d kn, join in third p of previously made ring, 2 d kn, join in second p of same ring, 2 d kn. Join in first p of next now of first row. 2 d kn. Close ring.

Turn work and make a bow of 3 times 2 d kn alternately with 2 p. Join in next p of same how as joined before. 3 d kn, 1 p, 3 d kn. Join in first p of following and last bow of center design. 2 d kn, 1 p, 2 d kn, 1 p, 2 d kn. Join in last p of following bow. Now repeat from ★ to end of row.

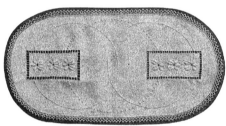

Oval Centerpiece With Tatted Edge

The oval centerpiece illustrated on this page measures nine inches in width and eighteen inches in length, not counting the tatted edge. The embroidered design is both unusual and effective, and, considering the space covered, there is very little work. The center one of the three interlaced circles is formed of satin-stitch dots placed about three-eighths of an inch apart, while the other two circles are made by working a row of Turkish stitch on the wrong side, leaving a space about one-eighth of an inch wide between the upper and lower row of stitches. On the right side this Turkish stitch shows up as two rows of tiny back stitches with the plain

linen between. The background of the two oblong motifs which complete the design is filled with seeding and on this the flowers, worked in split and plain satin-stitch, stand out in bold relief. The edge of the centerpiece is finished with plain rings of tatting joined to the edge of the linen with a crocheted beading.

The little luncheon napkin, shown on the same page, is simplicity itself and yet because of this very simplicity, it has a certain charm and style which more elaborate designs frequently lack. It measures eleven inches square, with each corner cut in about half an inch at a distance of two inches from the corner (see illustration). In each of the four corners is set a little wreath, slightly oval, the length measuring a bit more than the

A Unique Design for a Luncheon Napkin

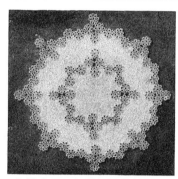

An Effective Centerpiece Made With Tatted Wheels

width and worked in an effective combination of satin-stitch and eyelet work. If desired, a tiny initial may be placed in one of the wreaths. The tatted edge is similar to the one on the oval centerpiece, only that it is joined directly to the buttonholed edge of the linen, with no crocheting between.

All of the embroidery on these two articles is done with the soft, lustrous Floss Embroidery Cotton, which comes in long skeins Nos. 6 to 40, while the tatting edges use Clark's Six Cord Crochet Cotton No. 70.

Housewives who are in need of serviceable breakfast or luncheon sets cannot do better than to make their centerpieces and doilies out of a coarse linen, trimming them with tatting. The directions for the centerpiece illustrated on this page follow and directions are also given for tatting for the edge of the doilies to match.

All of the wheels in the centerpiece are made in the same way, the effective design being obtained by simply joining them to form a pattern. Begin the center ring with 8 ds with a p between each 2 ds; draw up. Around this center ring make eight outer rings thus: 4 ds, 1 p, 2 ds, 1 p, 2 ds, 1 p, 2 ds, 1 p, 2 ds, 1 p, 4 ds, draw up and fasten in picot of center ring. In working the second and succeeding rings the picot after the 4 ds must be omitted and the stitch fastened into the fifth picot of the preceding ring.

The doilies to match this centerpiece may be finished around the edge with half-wheels of tatting made with the same thread as was used for the centerpiece.

Make the center ring of 18 ds with a p between each two stitches; draw up. Then begin the first of the five outer rings by making 4 ds, 1 p, 2 ds, 1 p, 2 ds, 1 p, 2 ds, 1 p, 2 ds, 1 p, 4 ds; draw up and fasten in picot on center ring. Make four more rings like this first one, only, after the first 4 ds have been made, omit the picot and instead fasten into the fifth picot of preceding ring. The half-wheels are joined together by omitting the third picot on the first outer ring of the second and succeeding half-wheels and fastening the stitch into the center picot of the fifth ring in the preceding half-wheel.

The very attractive collar and cuff set illustrated on this page, is edged with the little loops or wheels of tatting, while a simple motif fills in each corner of the collar.

A set like this is particularly suitable for use on children's coats or dresses and a very effective trimming for frocks of linen or chambray may be made by finishing the white collars and cuffs with the tatting edge, done with thread the same color as the dress.

In sewing the tatting on the collar, it is wise to first roll and whip the edge of the linen or batiste, afterward overhanding the loops of the tat-

Collar and Cuff Set Trimmed With Tatting

ting firmly to the edge of the material. Care must be taken, however, to see that the stitches are not drawn too tight, else the tatting will pucker and draw when the little dress is washed.

The tatting is done with one shuttle, first making the star in the center of the motif thus: Make 5 rings of 4 times 5 d kn alternated with 3 picots. Join the first and last ring together by means of the first and last picot; cut thread. ★ Knot thread on the joined picot between two rings. Make 5 d kn, join in the top picot of wheel and make three rings exactly like those made in the center star; cut thread and fasten. Repeat from ★ all around center star, making five three-petal groups in all.

For the corners of the cuffs only the center star of the motif was used (see illustration).

Knitting

Knitting is one of the oldest forms of needlework and is probably adaptable to more varied uses than any of the other crafts. One may use from two to five needles in making a knitted garment, and these needles may be of bone, steel, amber or wood, according to the thread one intends to use.

In knitting, the beginner should aim to work rather loose, so that the stitches will slip easily on the needle. If the thread is drawn too tight, it becomes difficult to pick up the stitches, especially when working with fine thread and steel needles.

To Cast On Stitches With One Needle—Hold the end of the thread under the third and fourth fingers of the left hand. With the right (which also holds the needle) bring the thread from under the left thumb up over it and also over the first finger of the left hand, then downward under the finger and up over the thumb (see Fig. 1). Next pass the point of the needle under the crossing and up back of that portion of the thread that is brought down from the first finger (see Fig. 2);

Fig. 1

draw it forward toward the left, grasp the crossing with the thumb and finger (see Fig. 3), throw the thread over the needle with the right hand (which holds the thread as in regular knitting), draw a loop through, slip the thread off the left first finger and draw it down to knot the stitch or loop on the needle. Repeat until you have the required number of stitches on the needle.

Plain Knitting (Fig 5)—The thumb and first finger of the right hand have the principal part of the work to do. The left hand keeps almost motionless. After casting on one row of stitches insert the right-hand needle into the front part of the first loop on the left needle, throw thread over left needle, as shown in Fig. 4 on page 83, drawing the thread through with the right needle and slipping off the loop or stitch from left needle.

To Purl (Figs. 6, 7, 8)—Throw the thread over in front of right-hand needle. Keep the first loop of the left needle near the point of the left needle. Take up the loop with right-hand needle by inserting the needle in front loop from back to front. Throw the yarn around the right needle, drawing the thread through to back, and at the same time let the loop or stitch slip from the left needle.

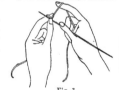

Fig. 2

Fig. 3

Fig. 4

To Decrease by Plain Knitting—Slip one stitch from needle, knitting next stitch plain and then draw the slipped-off stitch over the knitted stitch. This is the method to be employed in binding off or finishing a piece of knitting; the stitches are "knit and slipped" until there is only one stitch left on the needle; then the thread is broken and the end drawn through the last stitch.

To Decrease by Purl—Purl two loops off together.

To Increase—Make two loops out of one, working first one stitch in front loop, and then, by leaving stitch on left needle, another loop in the back thread of same loop. The same thing may be done when the row is purled.

Slip Stitch—Slip a stitch from one needle to the other without either knitting or purling it.

Directions for Knitting Holes. (Pattern illustrated on page 85)—Knit as many rows as are desired in plain knitting, then in the row where the holes are to be made knit five stitches plain then knit two together, five more plain, two more together and continue in this way to the end of the row. On the return row knit the five plain stitches, then throw thread over needle, five more stitches, thread over needle and continue in this way to end of row. Knit the next row plain, knitting the "thread over" stitches just like the others. The holes may be spaced farther apart if desired by simply knitting more plain stitches between.

Abbreviations Used in Knitting

K—Knit plain. P—Purl. N—Narrow. Sl—Slip stitch. O—Over.

★ Stars or asterisks mean that the directions given between them are to be repeated as many times as directed before going on with the directions which follow.

Symbols Used in Directions for Patterns on pages 86 and 87

■ Plain.

● Purl.

◢ Narrow by slipping one loop and knitting one. Draw slipped loop over knitted one.

◸ Narrow by knitting two loops together.

○ Thread over needle.

∨ Knit two loops out of one.

☐ Slip thread from one needle on to another.

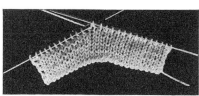

Fig. 5

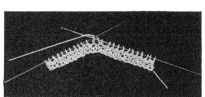

Fig. 6.   Purl—First Motion

Knitted lace is quite as durable as that which is crocheted, but as it takes a much longer time to knit a yard of edging or insertion than it does to crochet it, comparatively little knitted lace is made. The designs for knitted laces are always more fine and delicate than those to be carried out in crocheting, the patterns shown on page 87 being typical. The insertion and edging to match, pictured on page 87, would be especially attractive on pillow slips, bedspreads or bolster covers.

Fig. 7.   Purl—Second Motion

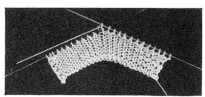

Fig. 8.   Purl—Third Motion

O.N.T.

Fancy Knitting Patterns

The pattern on the left shows the very popular border of two plain and two purl; and the pattern on the right is a fancy open mesh pattern done as follows:

Fancy Open Mesh Knitting Pattern

1st row—Kn plain.

2nd row—Purl.

3rd row—★ slip 1, knit 1, slip the slipped loop over the knitted one. Repeat from ★ to end of row, then repeat from first row and continue working in this way for length desired.

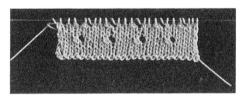

How To Knit Holes

Knitted Lace in Fine Thread

This very dainty lace in the smaller sizes is suitable for fine handkerchiefs, baby outfits, fine lingerie, etc. The larger model is the same pattern, and may be worked in any width by enlarging the pattern with cross-section paper.

O. N. T. 6 Cord Mercerized Crochet Cotton No. 60-100, and two Milward's Steel Knitting Needles No. 18 are used.

For the wide lace cast on 25 loops. For the smaller one 15.

By referring to the diagrams it will be seen that only the uneven rows are shown. The even rows are all done in plain knitting.

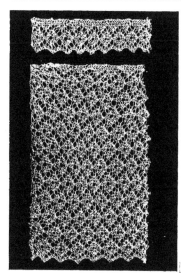

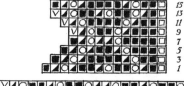

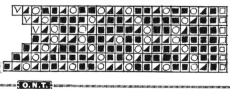

15 13 11 9 7 5 3 1

O.N.T.

Knitted Laces

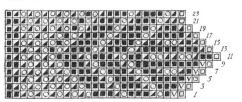

Even rows are knit plain. The explanation of the symbols used in these knitting diagrams is given on page 83.

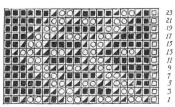

Weaving

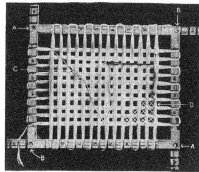

The Frame Assembled

A comparatively new form of needlework has been made possible in the last few years, by means of a small weaving frame which is adjustable to any size up to fifteen inches.

This frame before being assembled, consists of four sticks or sections exactly alike in size and shape, each section having twenty-six grooves or slots and a metal connector at one end. The figures from 4 to 15 on the top of each section indicate the number of inches to which the frame may be adjusted. The metal connectors provide a means of joining the various sections and thus forming a complete frame on which a net may be woven.

Each metal end or connector has a round hole in the center through which the numbers of the adjoining sections may be seen when the frame is being put together, thus making it a very simple matter to assemble the four parts accurately.

By means of this frame mats of almost any shape—round, square, oval, oblong or octagon—may be woven, and these in turn may be made into bags, runners, scarfs, sofa pillows, bedspreads and even into dainty little jackets or negligees.

Practically any kind of thread may be used on this frame, silk, cotton, wool or linen producing equally satis-

O.N.T.

factory results. Cotton, however, is more often used, the mercerized threads having quite as attractive an appearance as silk at a considerably lower cost and the numerous weights in which cotton threads may be bought make it suitable for practically every purpose.

Woven table mats are much newer and even more practical than the crocheted mats which have been popular for so many years. Crocheted mats always required an asbestos mat underneath, but when these woven mats are made with No. 3 Pearl Cotton or a very coarse mercerized thread it would be an exceptionally hot dish that would require an asbestos pad as well.

Although the frame will not make a piece of weaving larger than fifteen inches square, it is possible to make a centerpiece twenty-one or even twenty-seven inches in diameter by simply weaving it in four sections, joining them after the work is completed. Such a centerpiece is shown on page 91, this one being twenty-seven inches in diameter. For a piece of this size four large mats, made with the frame set 15 x 15, will be needed and one small 5 x 5 mat for the center. Use white or cream Pearl Cotton No. 5 or Spool Cotton No. 8, in either twelve, sixteen or twenty-four strands. Join the large mats together by their square

A Pretty Dressing Sack

sides; cut off all the fringe on the small mat except four threads at each corner, which may be used to tie this mat in the center hole of the large mat. Trim the fringe to the same length all around.

With this centerpiece should go six or more small mats or doilies eight inches in diameter to be used for bread and butter plates, or cups and saucers. The breakfast or luncheon plates will require nine-inch doilies while a

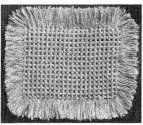

Mat To Put Under Hot Dishes

couple of oval mats, eight by ten or ten by twelve inches, should also be included in the set, to be placed under the platters or serving dishes to be used on the table.

Directions for putting the frame together or assembling the parts, as it is called, come with every frame that is sold so that there is no need for repeating them here, but it may be as well to give the foundation or groundwork for some of the more simple mats.

A square mat is, of course, the easiest to make, so we will begin with that. After the frame has been put together, start at one corner by tying the strand of thread in the first outside slot next to the metal connector or corner (see illustration of frame). Then run the strand through the first slot in the same section, to the right of the metal corner, then across to the corresponding slot in the opposite section; wind it around the outside of the dental in that direction, return through second slot in that section across the frame again through the corresponding slot and wind around the outside of the dental to point of starting. Repeat this operation eight times in the same slots, until there are eight strands across the frame from each slot. Then pass on to the next two slots and wind eight strands and continue winding in this way until all the slots have eight strands across the frame. Now pass the cord underneath the corner and run across the frame in directly opposite way, putting eight strands into each slot, same as on first side; then return to the first slots at right angles again, going completely across the frame three times each way until there are twenty-four strands in every slot.

The laid threads are now ready to be tied and this is done with a piece of the same thread put through the eye of a bodkin, coarse darning or tape needle. Begin at any corner, and pass the thread diagonally around the interwoven

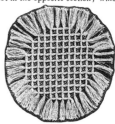

A Tumbler Doily

O.N.T.

strands at first intersection; draw tight and knot on underside of mat (see illustration of frame marked C); pass on diagonally to next intersection, again draw tight and knot on lower side or bottom of mat and continue in this way until all the strands have been tied one way. Then begin at corner marked B and work in the same way, and when this second row of diagonal threads has been tied, the mat is finished. To remove the mat from the frame push the latter apart at the corners and then slip the mat off the frame. Lighter weight and less expensive articles may be woven by making the mat of only eight or sixteen strands thickness. In order to make round, oval or octagon shape mats the weaving is done just as if a square mat was to be made, but when the knotting is begun the edge must be "stepped," some of the tying being done between the intersections. In anything but a square mat the outline is tied first, and afterward all the intersections, diagonally, both ways, within the outline.

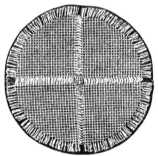

A Large Centerpiece

When larger articles, such as soft pillows, dresser scarfs or bedspreads, are to be made, it is necessary to join the squares together until the desired size is obtained. This joining is done by tying the uncut fringe loops of the mats together. Take, for instance, the centerpiece shown on this page. This is made of four mats fifteen inches square and one mat five inches square. When the mats were completed, two were laid, right side up, so that the fringe loops of one mat overlapped, or laid on top of, the loops of the other mat. Then the loops of the one mat were tied firmly to the edge or border of the other, by running a single thread of the same material through the loop and around the edge, tying firmly. When the one side was finished the mats were turned over and the other loops and edge tied together, afterward joining the third and fourth mats together and then the other two by the same method. After the large mats were joined the small center was inserted in the same way and the outer fringe cut and trimmed to an even length.

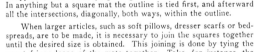

CROCHET

THE STANDARD THREAD FOR HAND AND MACHINE SEWING

6 CORD
MERCERIZED
CROCHET

Proper Thread Sizes for Various Materials

Heavy Woolens, Tickings, Bags, Heavy Coats, Trousers, Etc. Heavy Clothing generally.	Nos. 8 to 24
Tickings, Woolen Goods, Trousers, Boys' Clothing, Corsets, Cloaks, Mantles, Etc.	Nos. 24 to 40
All kinds of Heavy Calicoes, Light Woolen Goods, Heavy Silks, Seaming, Stitching, Dressmaking, Etc.	Nos. 30 to 50
Shirtings, Sheetings, Bleached Calicoes, Muslins, Silks, General Domestic Goods, and all Classes of General Work.	Nos. 50 to 70
Very fine Calicoes, Linens, Linen Shirtings, Fine Silk Goods, Etc.	Nos. 70 to 100
Very fine thin Muslins, Cambrics, Linens, Etc.	Nos. 100 to 200

CROCHET
& TATTING

"LUSTRE"

CROCHET
TWIST

DARNING

MERCERIZED
DARNING

O.N.T.

Concerning Clark's O. N. T. Articles

For many years Clark's O. N. T. Spool Cotton has been synonymous with "The best cotton thread." The ever-increasing world wide use of these threads, which are now made to suit every requirement for sewing, crocheting, embroidery, smocking, darning, tatting, and knitting, must be accepted as an eloquent tribute to their steadfast quality and merit.

The illustrations present the Clark's O. N. T. Cotton Threads now available throughout the country. A brief description is appended for your information and guidance.

Spool Cotton

Clark's O. N. T. Spool Cotton is the standard six cord sewing thread for hand and machine sewing. Three threads of two strands each are twisted into one, producing a six-cord thread unequaled for strength, elasticity and smoothness. There are two hundred yards on each spool, one dozen spools in each box. O. N. T. may be obtained in White and Black in sizes 8 to 200 and in one hundred and twenty staple colors in sizes 50 and 60. O. N. T. colors are used extensively on silk as well as on cotton fabrics.

Crochet Cottons

Clark's O. N. T. Crochet Cotton is the standard six cord cabled crochet, and is used for all kinds of crochet work when a plain finish is desired. The coarse sizes are used for bedspreads, pillow shams, etc. A steady demand for this plain crochet has continued regardless of the advent of mercerized cottons. There are two hundred yards on each spool, ten spools in each box. O. N. T. Crochet may be obtained in White in sizes 5 to 100, and in Black, Cream, Light Cream, Ecru, Turkey Red and Moss Green in sizes 30 to 50.

Clark's O. N. T. Crochet & Tatting Cotton is a superior quality of plain finish six cord crochet and tatting cotton, and is used for extra fine work. It is especially adapted for Irish and Venetian laces. There are two hundred and twenty yards to each ball, ten balls to the box. This quality is made in White only, sizes 30, 40, 50, 60, 70 and 80.

Clark's O. N. T. Crochet Twist is a six cord, hard twisted, plain finish crochet cotton, strong, smooth, elastic, and free from cnots, prepared specially for macing large pieces such as bedspreads, curtains,

centerpieces, table runners pillow shams and doilies. There are two hundred and twenty yards on each ball, sixteen balls to the box. It is made in White, Cream, Ecru and Arabian and in one size only, No. 5.

Clark's O. N. T. Six Cord Mercerized Crochet is a cabled or corded cotton of superior quality, excellent lustre and perfect smoothness. The medium sizes are used for general work, laces, edges, insertions, doilies, bags, belts, purses, shawls, slippers, etc.; the fine sizes for tatting, Irish and other fine crochet, and the coarse sizes for bedspreads, curtains, centerpieces, fringes, tassels and macrame work. The yardage per ball varies according to size, from 37 yards of No. 1 to 385 yards of No. 100. It is made in White and Ecru in sizes 1 to 100 and in a number of popular shades in the most desirable sizes.

Clark's O. N. T. "Lustre" Crochet Cotton is a two-ply medium-twisted mercerized cotton of excellent brilliancy and exceptional softness. Since its introduction several years ago its popularity has rapidly advanced. It is used for all kinds of crochet, embroidery, knitting and smocking. As a substitute for silk for general work it has no equal. There are one hundred yards on each spool, one dozen spools in each box. O. N. T. "Lustre" may be obtained in White, Black and sixty staple colors—one size only.

Darning Cottons

Clark's O. N. T. Darning Cotton is an eight-ply, four-end, loose-twisted cotton of exceptional softness. The strands may easily be separated, so that one to four may be used at a time. It is the standard cotton for darning and mending hosiery and undergarments. The White is used also as a foundation for initials, monograms and heavy embroidery. There are forty-five yards on each spool, one dozen spools in each box. O. N. T. Darning Cotton may be obtained in Black, White and sixteen staple colors.

Clark's O. N. T. Mercerized Darning Cotton is a four strand, loose-twisted thread, soft and pliable, for darning and mending silk, mercerized and lisle hosiery, undergarments, gloves, etc. The strands may easily be separated. There are forty-five yards on each ball, twelve balls to the box. It may be obtained in Black, White and sixteen staple colors.

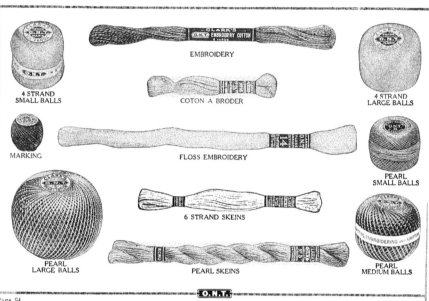

4 STRAND
SMALL BALLS

EMBROIDERY

COTON A BRODER

4 STRAND
LARGE BALLS

MARKING

FLOSS EMBROIDERY

PEARL
SMALL BALLS

PEARL
LARGE BALLS

6 STRAND SKEINS

PEARL SKEINS

PEARL
MEDIUM BALLS

O.N.T.

Embroidery Cottons

The excellent lustre, uniformity of color, size and twist of Clark's O. N. T. embroidery cottons make using them a delight, and, what is perhaps the most important feature, they are warranted to be absolutely fast if ordinary care is taken when laundering. They have been put up in various forms so as to meet the requirements of every class of art needlework.

Clark's O. N. T. Embroidery Cotton is a two-ply cotton of excellent lustre and exceptional softness. The White is made in sizes A, B, C, D, E and F in Hard Twist, and in three sizes, Coarse, Medium and Fine in Soft Twist. It is unequaled for working on flannel, linen, and white goods. The colors are made in a large range of well blended shades in two sizes, Rope and Floria, which come in Soft Twist only. The White is used for all styles of embroidery, but is especially adapted for Wallachian, Mount Mellick, eyelet, hardanger, hedebo, and solid embroidery. The colors in Rope size are used for conventional and floral designs on heavy material; in Floria size they are used with excellent results for conventional and floral designs. O. N. T. Embroidery Cotton is put up in varying yardages per skein, according to color and size.

Clark's O. N. T. Coton A Broder is a soft, round, medium twisted cotton of excellent lustre, and is used for cross stitch, French embroidery, shadow embroidery, filling, eyeleting, initialing, outline work, and punch work. There are twenty metres in each skein—about 22 yards, thirty-six skeins in each box. Clark's O. N. T. Coton A Broder may be obtained in White and a large range of nicely blending colors—the White in sizes 8 to 60; the Black and Colors in sizes 16, 25 and 35.

Clark's O. N. T. Floss Embroidery Cotton (Long Skeins) is a soft, loose-twisted, mercerized cotton, made in White only, and is used for French embroidery, shadow embroidery, eyeleting, scalloping, etc., but is especially adapted for initial work on handkerchiefs, napkins, doilies, and on extra fine materials. The length per skein varies from 55 to 109 yards according to size. Clark's O. N. T. Floss Embroidery Cotton may be obtained in sizes 6 to 60.

Clark's O. N. T. 6 Strand Cotton (Short Skeins) is a loose-twisted, mercerized cotton of excellent lustre and exceptional softness. The strands may easily be separated, so that from one to six may be used at a time. This feature makes the cotton adaptable for White and floral embroidery, cross-stitch, marking stitch, etc., on both light and heavy fabrics. It is particularly recommended for lingerie, handkerchiefs, and very fine work. There are eight metres in each skein—about 9 yards, twenty-four skeins in each box. Clark's O. N. T. 6 Strand Cotton may be obtained in White, Black, and a large range of nicely blending colors in one size only, No. 25.

Clark's O. N. T. 4 Strand Cotton (Small Balls) is a soft, loose-twisted cotton of excellent lustre and superior finish, used for embroidery, mending, and crochet work. The strands may easily be separated, making it suitable for general requirements, and especially for solid, outline, shadow work, cross-stitch, and for mending hosiery and underwear.

The Small Balls contain twenty-eight yards each, and are obtainable in White and a large range of nicely blending shades.

Clark's O. N. T. 4 Strand Cotton (Large Balls) is a soft, loose-twisted cotton of excellent lustre and superior finish, used for embroidery, mending and crochet work. The strands may easily be separated, outline, shadow work, cross-stitch, and for mending hosiery and underwear. The Large Balls contain fifty-six yards each, and are obtainable in White and Black only.

Clark's O. N. T. Marking Cotton is a plain finished, four-ply, medium-twisted cotton, especially prepared for marking and embroidery. The White is excellent for general embroidery work when a dull finish is desired. There are thirty yards on each spool, and twelve spools to the box. It is made in three colors, Turkey Red, White and Blue, and in six sizes, numbers 8, 10, 12, 14, 16 and 18.

Pearl Cottons

Because of its adaptability for various uses Pearl Cotton has rapidly grown in favor. Clark's O. N. T. Pearl Cotton is a two-ply, medium-twisted, mercerized cotton of excellent lustre and exceptional softness, and is used for all kinds of crocheting, embroidery, knitting and smocking. It is put up in four separate and distinct forms.

Clark's O. N. T. Pearl Cotton in Small Skeins is especially adapted for designs on heavy materials, outline work, cross-stitch, French knots, hardanger, scalloping, and for edges on wash cloths, etc. There are twelve skeins in each box, the length per skein being as follows: Size 3, 16 Yards. Size 5, 27 Yards. Size 8, 49 Yards. Clark's O. N. T. Pearl Cotton in Small Skeins may be obtained in White in sizes 3, 5 and 8, and in a large range of nicely blending colors in size 5 only.

Clark's O. N. T. Pearl Cotton (Small Balls) is put up by weight—10 grammes to the ball, ten balls in each box, and is used for all kinds of crochet work, embroidery, knitting and smocking. As a substitute for silk for general work it has no equal. Clark's O. N. T. Pearl Cotton Small Balls may be obtained in White, sizes 5, 8 and 12, and in a large range of nicely blending colors in size 8 only.

Clark's O. N. T. Pearl Cotton (Medium Balls) is put up by weight—20 grammes to the ball, ten balls in each box, and is used for knitting, crocheting and embroidering baby carriage-covers, baby jackets, slippers, afghans, shawls, bedspreads, centerpieces, table mats, doilies, laces, bags, purses, belts, etc. The White and Black are supplied in three sizes, Nos. 3, 5 and 8; the colors, of which there is a large range of nicely blending shades, may be had in two sizes, Nos. 3 and 5.

Clark's O. N. T. Pearl Cotton (Large Balls) is put up by weight—50 grammes to the ball, ten balls in each box, and is exactly the same as the medium balls, but it is especially adapted for making large pieces, as its use necessitates fewer knots. Clark's O. N. T. Pearl Cotton Large Balls may be obtained in the same colors and sizes as the Medium Balls.

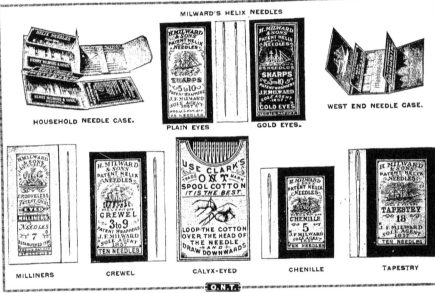

MILWARD'S HELIX NEEDLES

HOUSEHOLD NEEDLE CASE.

PLAIN EYES

GOLD EYES.

WEST END NEEDLE CASE.

MILLINERS

CREWEL

CALYX-EYED

CHENILLE

TAPESTRY

Henry Milward & Sons'
Accessories for Plain and Fancy Needlework

To obtain the best results, first class materials are absolutely essential. Your attention, therefore, is directed to the superior quality and excellent finish of the Needles, Crochet Hooks, Knitting Needles, and various other articles of Messrs. Henry Milward & Sons, Ltd., which are the result of more than one hundred years of experience. They are made of the best steel, by skilled workmen and by the most improved methods.

Milward's Calyx-Eyed Needles. This needle was made to meet a long felt want—that of a needle which could be threaded without any strain on the eyes. To thread the Calyx-Eyed Needle, the cotton is looped over the head of the needle and drawn downward, as shown in the illustration. They are made in two lengths, Sharps and Betweens, and are put up both in solid and assorted sizes, Nos. 1 to 9, ten needles to the paper.

Proper Needle Sizes for Clark's O. N. T. Spool Cotton

Clark's O. N. T. Spool Cotton Nos.	8	10	12	16-20	24-30	36-40	50-60	70-80	90-100	110-120	130-140	150-200
Milward's Needles Nos.	1	2	3	4	5	6	7	8	9	10	11	12

Needles for Hand Sewing

Milward's Helix Needles are made in three lengths, designated Sharps, Betweens and Ground Downs, in all sizes necessary for ordinary and special uses.

Milward's Gold Eye Needles. The eyes of these needles are burnished with gold, in order that they may be more easily threaded, particularly when used in an artificial light. They are made in two lengths, designated Sharps and Betweens, and in all sizes necessary for ordinary and special uses.

Milward's Milliners Needles are made both Plain and Gold Eyed. The particular feature of these needles is that they are extra long. They are made in all sizes necessary for ordinary and special uses.

Milward's Helix, Gold Eye and Milliners Needles are put up both in solid and assorted sizes, twenty-five needles to the paper.

Milward's Needle Books. These are obtainable in several sizes and qualities, the most popular being the "West End" assortment of two hundred and fifty needles, and the "Household" assortment of one hundred and fifty needles, both being intended for general requirements.

Milward's Glovers Needles are used for glove, fur and leather work. They are put up in solid sizes only, Nos. 1 to 8, twenty-five needles to the paper.

Needles for Embroidery

Milward's Crewel Needles are extensively used for all kinds of embroidery, and are much better adapted for the purpose than the ordinary sewing needle. They are put up in solid and assorted sizes, Nos. 1 to 12, ten needles to the paper, and twenty-five needles to the paper.

Milward's Chenille Needles are used for Chenille, Arrasene, Lace, and Embroidery work. They are made in solid and assorted sizes, Nos. 1 to 10, and are put up ten needles to the paper, and twenty-five needles to the paper.

Milward's Tapestry Needles are used for tapestry, rug, cross-stitch, and hardanger work. They are made in solid and assorted sizes, Nos. 17 to 28, and are put up ten needles to the paper, and twenty-five needles to the paper.

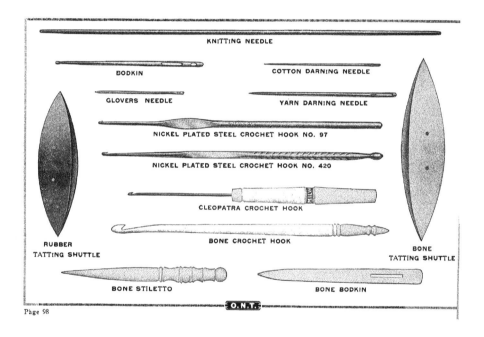

KNITTING NEEDLE

BODKIN

COTTON DARNING NEEDLE

GLOVERS NEEDLE

YARN DARNING NEEDLE

NICKEL PLATED STEEL CROCHET HOOK NO. 97

NICKEL PLATED STEEL CROCHET HOOK NO. 420

CLEOPATRA CROCHET HOOK

BONE CROCHET HOOK

RUBBER
TATTING SHUTTLE

BONE
TATTING SHUTTLE

BONE STILETTO

BONE BODKIN

O.N.T.

Needles for Darning

Milward's Yarn Darning Needles are made in solid sizes, Nos. 14 to 20, and are put up twenty-five needles to the paper. They are also put up in assorted sizes, 0 to 5, and 14 to 18, ten needles to the paper.

Milward's Cotton Darning Needles are made in solid and assorted sizes, Nos. 1 to 10, and are put up ten needles to the paper, and twenty-five needles to the paper. These are suitable for general work. For special uses there are also "Short" and "Double Long" lengths, ten needles to the paper.

Crochet Hooks

Proper Crochet Hook Sizes for Clark's O. N. T. Crochet Cottons

Clark's O. N. T. Crochet Cotton Nos.	1	3	5	10	15	20	25	30	40	50	60	70	80	100
Milward's Crochet Hooks Nos.	1	2	3	4	5	6	7	8	9	10	11	12	13	14

Proper Crochet Hook Sizes for Clark's O. N. T. Pearl Cotton

O. N. T. Pearl Cotton Nos.	3	5	8	12
Milward's Hooks Nos.	4	6	7	9

Milward's Nickel Plated Crochet Hooks No. 97. An attractive feature of this hook is the flat grip, which prevents the hook from turning when in use and gives perfect control in working. They are made in fourteen sizes, Nos. 1 to 14, and in two lengths, five inches and six inches.

Milward's Nickel Plated Crochet Hooks No. 420—Round Steel Handle— are made in fourteen sizes, Nos. 1 to 14.

Milward's Cleopatra Crochet Hooks—Bone Handle— are made in fourteen sizes, Nos. 1 to 14.

Miscellaneous Articles

Milward's Knitting Needles are made in eleven sizes, Nos. 12 to 22, and may be obtained singly or in sets of five.

Bone Crochet Hooks. These are made entirely of bone and in two lengths, five inch and six inch. The five inch may be had in six sizes, 0 to 5, and the six inch in seven sizes, 0 to 6.

Bodkins or Tape Needles are obtainable in Bone and Steel, and in one size only.

Stilettos. These are made of Bone, and are obtainable in three sizes, Nos. 1, 3, and 5.

Tatting Shuttles. These are obtainable in Bone in a medium size, and in Rubber in two sizes, large and medium.

O.N.T.